MW01126133

TYLER KICHAKUSUN

JUGGLING
BULLIES

Illustrations by Pio Tendero
Cover Design by Pio Tendero

Printed in the United States.

Paperback: 978-1-7365316-0-0
Hardback: 978-1-7365316-3-1
Ebook/Epub: 978-1-7365316-1-7

Library of Congress Control Number: 2022901173

DEDICATION

To those who have found the strength
to share their story,
and to those still seeking to find it.

Never ever give up on yourself or your dreams
For everything good in life is possible.

—Eva Mozes Kor

PROLOGUE

Silence flooded the room as the doors clicked and echoed behind the teachers. Only the spotlights beamed down on the wooden floor of the stage. Everyone looked around sheepishly to see who would break the ice and walk up to the

mic and begin speaking. I was running out of time, as if I were standing in an hourglass, sand closing in around me. If I didn't speak my mind soon, I would be buried too deep to move. My heart raced as I considered being that person. What would I say if I could gather the gumption to go up there?

After all, I had spent my entire high school life trying to disappear, and now I had to be seen and heard, even open up to classmates in deep conversation.

The truth is I would have rather died than give the people who hurt me more ammunition to use against me in the future. But in the end, how it turned out shaped my life in the years to follow. And now, as an adult, I look back still in complete awe about what happened.

The retreat began with the entire senior class of more than a hundred boys in one room singing songs. I mean, they sang, and I stood there motionless with my mouth shut tight as I clenched my jaw. Many of my smiling classmates were buying into the kumbaya moment, but my heart and mind had been damaged too much to believe any of this could help me feel better. If I chose to sing, it wouldn't take away the hurt. I would need to do something totally different, something powerful and memorable.

The senior class was in this auditorium for about an hour, but it quickly transitioned into small groups of eight to ten boys. My heart started beating heavily in my chest and then grew to my temples and even my fingertips. Each group walked the campground to find the perfect spot to circle up and huddle in for some serious conversations. My stomach was turning inside out even though I was lucky enough to only have four boys in my group. Some of them were a part of my long-term pain, and it was enough to make me collapse into my shell.

The teacher prompted, "Let's go around the circle and say something we are grateful for about our classmates."

This was my worst nightmare. I didn't have anything to say. As the round-robin conversation proceeded, the other boys shared.

One in particular mentioned, "They're not in this group, but I am so lucky to have met five of my best friends at this school. I don't know what I would've done without them. They've been there for me when I almost felt like quitting on life, yet they stepped in and encouraged me when I needed it most."

Oh, wow. Well, that was really nice.

I was honestly happy he was able to find true friendship and support here, except I would never be able to utter anything remotely the same. I was on my own lifeboat trying to find my way to land, while on his, he had all five of his friends along the treacherous journey through high school.

When it got to me, I just shook my head and mumbled under my breath, "I'm not ready." I didn't really have that many friends at school, and I would have lied if I said, "I am so thankful for all of my classmates." Most of my peers didn't even really know who I was besides another body in their classrooms.

Thank goodness that was now finished so we could have our break and get to the final event, Open Mic. Everyone poured into the open room. Many boys were reuniting with their friends after having been split up during the breakout sessions.

Over the microphone, a teacher announced, "Alright, boys. Find a spot on the floor."

"Hey, let's go sit over here," reverberated around the room, yet it was never directed toward me. I surveyed the tightly filled area and plopped down on the hard carpet with enough space to spread my legs out in front of me and stretch my arms backward with my palms on the ground.

As the room turned to faint whispers, one teacher addressed the students. "This is Open Mic. Anyone may come onstage at any time during this event and say anything he wants to the senior class. Yes, anything. Also, all of the teachers are going to leave the room."

Utter shock overcame us as most were not expecting to be left completely alone. After only a minute of listening to the instructions, here we were, the entire senior class, sitting in almost complete darkness, wondering what would happen next.

As I sat there planning my speech inside my head, there was movement from the side of the room. One brave soul slowly made his way onto the stage. Impressed by his courage, we all held our collective breath to hear what he had to say.

In those few seconds just before he spoke, I wondered why I didn't have the backbone to go up on stage, grab the mic, and profess my truth? Instead, I sat frozen and lifeless, barely breathing as I anticipated what he would say.

Maybe I should have; I really wanted to. But I wouldn't. After all, I was sitting with the very people who had made my life a living hell. I had plenty to say to them—lots to get off my chest. I could have given them an earful for sure.

Gosh, just do it. No. No, you can't do it. I heard the voices inside my head fighting. What happened next surprised everyone.

CHAPTER 1

I t was the summer before kindergarten and about ninety degrees outside, but I thrived in that kind of weather. The sun was low in the sky, partially hidden behind scrubby live oak trees. The sweat beads on my forehead dampened my short sleeves as I wiped them. Being outdoors and doing something active was much preferred above sitting stagnate indoors. So when my older sister Michelle had a T-ball game one early evening, I declared, "I'm coming!" I knew I would get to run around and play while she reluctantly participated with her team.

Michelle begged, "Mom, can Tyler please play in my place? I don't even like T-ball. It doesn't even make sense."

"Sweetheart, it's girls only. Don't you want to spend some time with your friends?" Mom said.

"Ugh. Yes, but not while hitting a silly ball off of a standing tube. Also, it's too hot outside! I don't wanna . . ."

"Michelle, we are going, and you are participating."

"C'mon guys, let's go," I shouted.

Michelle was two years older than me, but she highly disliked sports and physical activity. Her games were at the local parks and recreation center and the best part about it was the nearby playground. I'm sure my mom was just as grateful it was there to keep me occupied.

Surrounded by chain-link fencing, this area was heaven for little kids like me with endless possibilities to jump, swing, climb, and potentially make my mom constantly peer over hoping I wasn't being too daring. I wasn't a very bold child anyhow, so I'm not sure why she even looked. Early on I developed a low tolerance for taking high risks because we were a rule-following family.

This evening, for the first ten minutes, I had the whole playground to myself. Grabbing and swinging from the monkey bars, I sometimes skipped a bar or two to see how far I could reach. When I got to the other side, I swayed back and forth a couple times to build up my speed before letting go and flying in the air, smushing the grass beneath my shoes as I landed while catching the rest of my body with my hands. After regaining my balance, I walked over to the sandbox where I dug and tried to build an epic sand castle without water. Despite the beads of sweat dripping down my back, I enjoyed my creation and getting to do whatever I wanted.

My sister and I didn't typically play together very often, so I was used to entertaining myself in isolation. She was an adult in a child's body who asked for a sip of coffee in the morning to start her day rather than watch cartoons. Like many young children, I longed for somebody with whom I could run around, build towers out of blocks, throw or kick a ball in the yard, or swim all day.

SQUEAK.

The gate of the playground opened behind me. A small breeze blew some sand in my eyes, and I quickly tried to use the sides of my pointer fingers to get it out. That didn't help much, so I lifted the bottom of my shirt to use as a rag. As I was blinking heavily and everything was coming back into focus, a large shadow grew over the sandbox.

"Hey. Wanna play?"

Two boys around my age were standing tall right behind me, one of them a little bigger than the other. It was the smaller one who had the much larger personality. If I was a not-so-audacious child, then this boy fit the mold of a risk taker.

His name was Gene.

As we ran around the playground together, he began to subtly tell everyone what to do.

"Hey, let's go play on the swings!"

"Okay!"

So we played on the swings.

"Hey, let's go on the slide now!"

"Okay!"

Boy, was I having fun with my new friends! Heck, this beat doing the same old boring stuff by myself.

"Let's go on the monkey bars!"

I followed suit. Gene would lead, and I would follow. On the swings, we had to do it his way.

"Hey, let's see who can let go and land the farthest! I'll go first."

I hesitated. "I'm not sure . . ."

Without listening, he'd smile and exclaim, "Okay, your turn!"

As I tried to turn on the power button to my bravery, I had the wimpiest leap while landing well short of Gene's spot; but of course, he was happy because he won.

After that, he'd announce, "Last one to the top of the slide is a rotten egg!" With a head start before finishing his statement, he was already looking down at me, grinning and laughing. We were just having fun, right? I continued to quickly climb my way to the top of the slide because we were just playing. I thought that's what friends did. Perched atop and gazing down at Gene, I had no idea I was following him into the abyss.

Gene's friend proposed another activity, and Gene acknowledged it but swiftly said something like, "No, let's . . ." and somehow, we managed to do whatever Gene suggested every time.

I had not noticed he had chosen everything we would do on that hot and dry playground, but still, I was satisfied because I had made a new friend, and guess what? I found out he was going to the same school as me that fall, a local private school. And like me, he also was going into kindergarten.

My mom's voice echoed in the distance, "Tyler! It's time to go!"

"Bye, Gene. I gotta go. I'll see you later."

Still full of energy, I half skipped and half ran back over to my mom.

She smiled at me. "C'mon. The game is over. We're going to pick up some dinner on the way home."

We had a magical time on the playground that hot summer day, but I had no idea the simple act of Gene singularly choosing our playground activities would begin to define the rest of my adolescent life.

CHAPTER 2

My mother was raised in a strict home, and she attended private schools. So when she and my father married, they decided to raise their children in the same way. We would go to church as a family, and I went to private schools, just like my mother. This meant strict rules and uniforms were in my near future.

I remembered walking into school on the first day of kindergarten. I stood outside the doorway with a knot in my stomach, but once I passed that threshold, I could see all my new classmates, and everyone seemed to be having so much fun as they smiled and laughed.

A sweet older lady with gray hair and red-rimmed glasses was smiling from ear to ear. "Hi, Tyler! Good morning! I'm Mrs. Kay. Welcome to our classroom! You're going to have so much fun. Come on over here and put your stuff down." She guided me through the room with her hand on my shoulder.

"Vroom!" A couple of boys were rolling a car down a large ramp, and life seemed amazing.

"My turn now!" another boy called out.

"Boys, don't get too loud now, okay?" Mrs. Kay still had a twinkle in her eye.

As I scanned the room, I saw a couple kids reading an animal picture book together in the corner. Some girls were building tall structures with multi-colored blocks, and a small group of boys were creating a make-believe scene with superhero action figures and cars.

Still with a bit of butterflies in my stomach, I had an uneasiness about meeting these new kids. This was my first time in a real school, and I hoped I would make some friends. The room was full with over a dozen students, a mixture of boys and girls, but instead of experiencing walking into this place together on day one, it was like they had all started without me. For a moment, I considered crying for my mom, but then I heard something familiar.

"Hey! Let's play with this."

"Yeah! Okay!"

Then I suddenly realized, the voice was my new friend from the T-ball playground, and he was in my kindergarten class! Gene! He was there! I was so excited because I didn't know anyone else in the room, so it was nice to have my new friend in the class. My eyes lit up and the butterflies left my body.

Gene was slightly hidden behind a small bookshelf. He and two other boys were all sitting together in tiny plastic blue chairs tossing a ball to each other.

Mrs. Kay encouraged me. "Go ahead, Tyler. Go have some fun." She patted me on my back and gave me the smallest nudge like she knew I needed it.

Without confidently making eye contact, I slowly went over to Gene and grabbed a seat. They continued throwing to each other. "Hey, catch!" One of the boys pitched it to me underhanded. After flipping it back to Gene, he asserted, "This is boring. Let's do something else. Hey, follow me. There's another set of race cars over here."

"Oh, yes!" One of the other boys immediately approved the suggestion.

This is what everyone seemed to do around Gene. Kids in general already tried to one-up each other with the best toy or the best idea for an activity, but once Gene became a part of those conversations, nobody realized they were falling into the trap of a master manipulator, even at such a young age. When it came to who was the best or who had the best anything, I didn't care because all I wanted was for everyone to be happy.

Flashes of our time spent on the playground came back to memory quickly. I didn't understand why Gene seemed to want to control everything. So many things lacked his approval, but he was fun and laughed a lot. I wanted to be a part of the joy others were experiencing. Since very little received his acceptance, it was like so many people, including myself, were attempting to seek and find it.

Since I was the baby of the family, my sister usually got things before I did. I developed a bit of selflessness instead of jealousy because I learned early on that I wasn't always going to get what I wanted. I wouldn't be allowed to sit in the big chair at the kitchen table or sleep in the big bed at night, but I was okay with it. That mixed with my mother's strictness made me into a people pleaser, and I wanted others to be happy getting what they wanted first.

My classmates knew if they united with Gene, they might be making some small sacrifices, but they were going to have a great time.

"Zoom! Crash! Screech! I told you guys this was way better," Gene said, simultaneously making sure everyone was having a blast.

"I know! This is awesome!" I agreed.

Gene enjoyed my reassurance, and since I accommodated his recommendations, he accepted me as a friend.

As the school year progressed, I found myself trying to impress Gene more and more. It was almost as if being his friend gave me self-worth. There was just one problem, and it was a big problem. To impress Gene meant getting into trouble a lot in school. And what this meant was taking the blame for things he did wrong, and going to the principal's office to answer for the troublemaking behavior.

For example, I would do something in front of the class to make him and everyone else laugh, but then I got in trouble.

Gene could throw a wad of paper at somebody's back and snicker about it while making sure everybody saw except the teacher. When everyone laughed, it gave me the grand idea to chuck an even bigger paper ball across the room, yet when nobody laughed, I realized it was because the teacher was glaring right at me and walking over to change my card to red because of my actions.

But when Gene did the same thing, he slithered out of it, never getting punished. I kept making poor choices because of my desire to maintain his approval because it validated me in some pathetic way.

It's hard to believe as an innocent kindergartner I could feel such external pressure to fit in, but I did.

Have you ever heard of peer pressure?

In private schools, classes were small with twelve to sixteen students in a classroom. So imagine being in a small class with one student exerting his strong personality over the half dozen boys in the room. There was nowhere to hide. The only way to survive was to blend in with the crowd.

All the boys trying to survive began to act like the crowd's self-appointed leader, Gene, doing their best to one-up each other. Even though I was one of those followers, I still felt like I was an observer watching what he did and listening to what he was saying to everyone else. I was like a hidden camera taking in all of this footage and keeping it on a memory disk that never seemed to have the ability to become full. A camera doesn't react; it simply records, and my mind was recording what was happening. It would replay the recordings without me ever pushing play, and it seemed to do that often so that I could review the tape.

Gene's words subconsciously sank into my daily thoughts causing me to make choices to gain his approval. Gene hadn't approved of much, making this process that much harder.

He asked me, "Tyler, do you want to play tag?"

"No. Can we play on the swings instead?" I replied.

"Oh, c'mon. Let's play tag. You're it!" He danced around me waiting for me to reach out and tag him. Eventually I did, and we had a great time chasing each other, but I had no idea the dynamic developing in front of me was one where my opinion didn't truly matter. We never did go to the swings. I was the ultimate recipient of master manipulation, but so were many others. At such a young age, it was too difficult for me to identify what was happening, but inside my head, I was trying to analyze and interpret the best ways to handle this evolving situation. There was a hope and a belief in my heart we couldn't go on for very much longer until he might say, "Yeah! Great idea, Tyler! Let's do it!"

When we got to first grade, my behavior resulted in being sent to the principal's office. I was kicked out of class one day. The teacher made me stand in the hallway.

"Get out! I'm done with this." She pointed to the door.

I don't remember what I did, but I'm sure I was being disruptive. To make things worse, instead of sitting or standing in the hallway like a good student, I thought to myself, "What would Gene approve of in this situation?"

Keep in mind, Gene was not in my first-grade class, so why did I care what he thought? Anyhow, I decided to make faces through the window of the door to try and get the class to laugh. I also pulled the sides of my mouth open wide with my fingers and stuck my tongue out. Then I gently placed my lips on the glass only to exhale with force and make my cheeks blow up like balloons while opening my eyes really big. You can only imagine how that went over with my already displeased teacher.

How do I even remember Gene wasn't in my class? It was the way he bragged about his.

"We have the coolest teacher. You don't even know. Our class is by far the best."

This was Gene's mantra, and he mentioned it all the time. So I began to believe my class really wasn't as good as his, and my teacher wasn't as nice or as awesome, or at least that's what the recorded footage in my mind made me think as it would replay on a loop, almost brainwashing me.

Before I knew it, second grade had begun, and for the second year in a row, I was not placed in the same class as Gene. You know what that meant? The administration knew we were bad for each other and were purposely keeping us apart.

This happened in schools. Teachers talked about what was best for their students, and they obviously knew Gene and I were like Batman and Robin but not in a positive, impactful way. My job was to support what he wanted to do, not to share how I truly felt about anything, yet by doing this, I was causing more trouble than I realized. When I fulfilled that role, it made him happy, and since I enjoyed pleasing others, it was my natural instinct. There wasn't an ounce of understanding I was simultaneously building up Gene's ego as well as his power. Ultimately, the school assisted in dissolving a portion of this dynamic by having us remain in separate classes.

But if you were to ask Gene why we were apart, it was because I was not in the cool class, again. I knew it sounded silly, but his words really sank in. I believed, without a doubt, Gene's teacher, his class, and his classmates were superior to mine in every way.

It was in the second grade when I developed my first real crush on a girl named Susan. My insides fluttered with butterflies when she was nearby, but they were the good kind. Even my parents knew I was smitten over her, and they buttered me up and encouraged me to keep liking Susan.

Unfortunately, she wasn't the type of girl who would just tell me to go away, and I wasn't the type of boy who would roll over and give up easily, so I kept trying.

I genuinely had a crush on her and thought she was super cute. Her smile was as sweet as honey with her precious rosy cheeks and perfect shoulder-length haircut with a pretty white bow. Even though I was only in second grade, I decided I was going to ask her to be my girlfriend, not once, but twice. I was rejected, both times.

Toward the end of the school year, we had our annual field day. I noticed a girl had gotten a heart painted on her cheek with a boy's name inside of it. *Hey! What a great idea! She will love it!* I imagined being noticed by Susan.

"Oh, Tyler! You did this for me? Aw, how cute. That's so sweet." Her face blushed as she batted her eyelashes at me and smiled with her cute little bow in her hair.

"I really like you, Susan, and I know you already said no, but I hope you will give me a chance."

"Third time's a charm, Tyler. How could I say no to this?" She smiled and hugged me, and my heart skipped a beat.

When I snapped out of my daydream, I had the bristles with bright red paint sliding along my cheek as it curved around the top right side of the heart to the point on the bottom and then again on the left. With a bit smaller tipped brush, the kind parent volunteer gracefully painted Susan's name inside the heart on my cheek. It was perfect. I knew she would love it.

"Who is Susan?" The parent raised her eyebrows.

"She's going to be my girlfriend someday," I said.

"That is the cutest thing I have ever heard. So you are hoping she sees this?"

"Definitely. Then maybe she will get one with my name too."

"Well, I hope she likes it. I think you're good to go. Check it out." She held up the mirror.

I leaned in close and turned slightly to the side to get a better view. Then I sprung out of the chair and began looking for my sweet angel.

"Good luck with Susan!" the lady shouted.

I turned around looking over my shoulder. "Thank you!"

"That is so sweet," she murmured. "Okay. Who's next?"

My chest puffed out and I held my chin high. People were beginning to notice my bold artwork. At first, I was encouraged because I was putting my heart on my sleeve, I mean cheek. Whatever, I was being courageous in my own decision. Things took a turn when all the smiles slowly grew into laughter, but I didn't understand why.

When Gene and his friends saw, they made fun of it.

"Wow. Are you serious, Tyler? Guys, look at this! Oh my goodness."

Another student assisted as he rolled his eyes and laughed. "Susan is going to fall in love with you now that you painted her name on your face. Am I right?"

"Hey! There she is now. Let's show her. Susan! Susan! Over here!" They all shouted for her and pointed at my face. My chin was a bit lower now but still hopeful.

Gene and everyone were laughing with their hands over their mouths.

Susan glanced our way and squinted her eyes to see what they were snickering about when suddenly she saw it. Her eyes that were bright and beautiful began filling with tears.

The next thing I knew, Susan was running into the girl's bathroom crying. My face turned about as red as the paint, but it wasn't because of embarrassment for myself; it was the guilt of feeling like I had hurt her when I was only trying to profess my true love. Oh wait, I forgot second graders aren't really in love. Susan's closest friends ran into the bathroom to be with her as she cried. They stayed in there long enough that I left before they came back out.

Looking back, it was a risky move, not for what might have happened with Susan, but because it was abnormal for me to do something on my own without thinking about what Gene thought I should do.

That might have been one of the last times I followed through with an idea of mine, without worrying what Gene was going to think or say about me. Everyone has things they want in life from small goals to big dreams, and when somebody else like Gene steps in preventing people like me from even mentally taking a step toward their own aspirations because of strong opposing opinions, it can eventually chip away and break down one's belief in their own decisions. When Gene laughed and asked if I was serious, my natural reaction was to respond, "No, Gene. C'mon. I am just messing around." In reality, my heart was saying, "Actually, I am serious, but it doesn't seem like I should tell you because you obviously have an issue with the decision I have made."

Which leads us to third grade. This was a big year for me. My mom, a very strict mother, was fed up with my behavior and getting phone calls from my teachers. Without even raising her voice, she put the fear in me with a simple look and a short statement. "Tyler, I need to talk to you."

Back when I was in preschool, she bribed me by saying if I

could be good for the entire week, and if the teacher could confirm it each Friday, then I was rewarded with a trip to Chuck E. Cheese! Oh man, Skee-Ball. That was my favorite game. I think I earned only one of those outings. All the other times, my mom or dad would show up at the end of the week, and I would be in timeout. I knew as soon as I slipped up even just one time, there was no getting my reward.

"But Mom. Please! I was good all week," I begged.

In the calmest but still serious motherly voice, "Tyler. You had to sit in time out. We are not going to Chuck E. Cheese. You can try again next week."

There was never any bartering success. Mom was always right. Crying and screaming never got me anything except sent to my room, so there was no sense in fighting it.

So when things were still heading south in third grade, my mom walked into my room one evening and said, "Tyler, we are having a meeting with your teacher after school tomorrow." She never tried hiding why, and she remained in a composed manner. "We are not going to be getting negative phone calls this year, so we are going to discuss a plan so that you can improve and start listening better in class."

"Yes, ma'am," I responded.

At the conference the next day, my mom brought a pack of red bookmark-sized cards that said "Great job this week" on them. She asked my teacher to monitor my behavior each week, and whenever I had a good one, to send me home with one of those cards. The teacher raised her eyebrows in surprise but then smiled. "Hmm. I like this. Thank you. Of course we can try this.

Fingers crossed it will help Tyler."

Thank you, Mom, because those cards changed my behavior. This helped me take a positive turn. No longer did I make it to the end of a long week of school and mess it all up with a silly mistake. At the end of most weeks, my teacher click-clicked over to me in her high heels and leaned over my desk, set down the bright red card, and slid it over in front of me with her index finger. She smiled big enough to see all her white teeth, and she whispered, "Great job this week, Tyler." Then, she gave me a light pat of affirmation on the back as she walked away. I learned to appreciate those kind, positive comments, and I had a desire to continue receiving them when I could.

Despite this new trend of success, I still worried about impressing Gene, but he wasn't in my homeroom, so I could manage to get by without getting in trouble.

Third grade was also the year I mastered juggling. The new physical education teacher thought it would be cool to introduce juggling to all students.

I can remember everyone having tissue-like pieces of semi-transparent cloth that floated in the air like feathers. They were training wheels because they moved so slowly through the air that it was easy to learn the process of throwing and catching them.

Once the basic concept of learning how the different items moved through the air was accomplished, it was time to move on to tennis balls. I practiced at home for hours on end. Two in my right hand, one in my left. I'd toss one from the right hand diagonally upward toward my left shoulder. As soon as I let go of the first ball in my right hand, I had to toss the one from my left hand so that it could cut through the invisible line drawn between my right hand and the first ball. Now, this was the moment of truth. The second ball was rapidly falling toward my right hand, but milliseconds before catching it, my brain had to learn to throw the last ball into the air while immediately catching and throwing the first ball back into the air to the opposite side. This was very difficult at the beginning. Toss, toss, toss, drop, drop, drop. Ugh. Toss, toss, toss, catch and toss, drop, drop, drop. Ugh!

"Tyler! Are you okay? What are you doing?" Mom belted from the living room.

"Yes, Mom! I'm practicing juggling! Ugh!" I hollered back.

"Excuse me? You better watch your tone, young man."

"Sorry, Mom. I'm just frustrated. I'm going to get this."

One day, while in P.E. class, the teacher introduced us to the Master Juggler Test, a series of juggling combinations to be performed by a count of ten consecutive cycles, while seamlessly transitioning from one combination to the next. If you stopped or dropped a ball, you failed.

I was determined to see if I could master this new juggling challenge. What ensued was endless hours of being locked away in my room doing nothing but juggling.

My mom, amazed with my newfound pastime, occasionally peeked in on me to make sure I was okay. What began as a few days, turned into weeks of practice. No longer was I experiencing toss and an immediate drop. I was on a whole new level now at toss, toss, toss and catch, toss and catch, toss and catch forever and ever until the cycle changed to a different rhythm or until I dropped one.

Let me remind you I was only eight years old and a third grader at the time.

Much to my surprise, there were times when I was in my room practicing the official cycle for the Master Juggler Test, and I successfully completed it! I got so excited, but my inner voice quickly reminded me I wasn't going to be able to prove to anyone I had accomplished it.

It's hard to believe, but cell phones hadn't even existed yet, so there was no way to record myself for proof. Instead, I quickly ran out of the room to ask my sister or parents to watch me do it again. Every time I tried it in front of them, I failed.

Even so, my dad took me to a special store where he bought an official juggling set for me to use, the kind you'd see in the circus with yellow, red, blue, and green balls. It made me feel loved that he supported me in this endeavor.

I was becoming good at something, but Gene didn't know. He was too busy doing his usual thing.

One day, I went to the P.E. teacher to tell her I was ready for her to watch me perform the Master Juggler Test. A friend went with me as a witness because he had been trying to pass the test too.

The teacher began with some reminders. "Boys, each time you make it through a single cycle of one-two-three, that counts as one. Each cycle must reach a count of ten before moving to the next sequence. Do not stop prior to transitioning to the following series of throws, or it will not count. Also, if you drop the ball even once, you fail. You may attempt the test up to two times maximum, and you are always allowed to come back another day and try again if necessary. Good luck to both of you. I know you have been practicing very hard."

As I began, it was like second nature because I had spent so much time preparing. I tossed three in a continuous cycle without skipping a beat. I juggled two in my right while the third rested in my left and effortlessly mirrored the same on the other side without stopping. Everything was going so smoothly, and I felt like a professional. I easily made it past halfway through the test before suddenly seeing one ball miss my hand and drop to the floor in slow motion. *Thud*. It landed on the floor. My wide eyes looked at the teacher and my mouth hung open.

"It's okay, Tyler. You did good. Try one more time. I know you can do it."

I quickly tried it a second time but did even worse. I was so embarrassed. This was how I learned to react because I was growing into a person who tried to impress others. Therefore, when I was unable to do this according to where the bar was set, I believed I hadn't succeeded when I should have told myself how great a job I had done because many others did not have the ability to juggle like I could at such a young age. My head hung low and my shoulders sagged as I dragged my feet back to class. It was back to practicing in my room to regain my confidence.

Maybe for me, juggling was something I could do in isolation and not be publicly ridiculed. I could relish in my own success without worrying what Gene or anyone else thought.

After just a couple more days of practice, I returned to the P.E. teacher.

She saw me approach her. "Tyler, you're back! Are you ready? I know you can do it!" She clapped her hands together to pump me up.

"Let's do it. I think I can." I shrugged my shoulders.

"I know you can!" she declared with strong belief.

Those simple words helped me truly have faith I could do it. Encouraging words meant something to me.

Internalizing those words, I closed my eyes and took a deep breath and imagined one toss after the other, methodically catching everything. Then, I opened my eyes and began.

This time I attempted the juggling test just once in front of her and passed! It was an incredible feeling, to be so young and to become a real Master Juggler. She even gave me my official certificate of achievement in front of the entire student body of kindergarten through eighth grade at a school-wide assembly in the gym.

"May I please have your attention," she said as she quieted everyone. Then she leaned into the microphone. "This year all of you were introduced to juggling, but only some of you rose to the challenge of trying to become a Master Juggler. Today, I want to recognize two students who achieved this great feat."

My heart was warm with joy, and I was proud of myself in this moment.

She continued, "First, I would like to reward . . ."

Everyone applauded. The boy from sixth grade strode up to the podium to accept his certificate.

"Now, out of all the students from kindergarten through eighth grade, our youngest to attempt the test is only in the third grade! This person worked so hard, and I couldn't be more proud. I would like to present the Master Juggler certificate to Tyler Richardson!"

A good rush ran through my body.

As she handed me the certificate, she smiled. "I knew you could do it, Tyler."

This experience taught me dedication and hard work truly pay off. The P.E. teacher's words stuck in my head: "I know you can!" I wanted to tell myself, "Yes! I can! I can juggle! I can do a lot of things!" I knew this was true, but then the hidden camera footage in my mind mixed with some false notions showed me a clip of Gene saying, "Wow. Are you serious, Tyler? Juggling? Oh my gosh." I tried pushing delete, but it always came back to me.

On the positive side, not only had I acquired a new skill, but I had also gained some notoriety and new friends who had also attempted the journey to become Master Jugglers.

Just around the corner was the talent show, so of course I thought, *Hey, I can juggle, why not do that? I am clearly a Master Juggler, so nobody could make fun of me, right? Wrong! Gene could make fun of me. His friends could make fun of me.* Or at least those were the thoughts running through my mind as I continued my daily practice sessions in my room.

But the talent show was still a whole month away, so I signed up because my juggling buddies had decided we would do an act together as a team. I was totally cool with that because it meant there would be strength in numbers. If we performed together, the spotlight wouldn't be directed solely on me, and they couldn't make fun of all of us, right?

We began with numerous practice sessions, but as we progressed, I became more and more nervous. I kept imagining people laughing at us in the crowd because we "couldn't" juggle, even though I knew we could. It was an internal battle. It was like I was juggling bullies in my mind.

"Look at them." They laughed and pointed.

"Wow. I know. Juggling." Shaking their heads.

"They're not even good."

"Juggling is for clowns."

I needed to believe in myself and my abilities and not what Gene or any other human on earth might say, but even though I was only in the third grade, I had been hearing comments like these about other people for the last four years of my life. Gene was always on one shoulder spreading negativity outward about others eighty percent of the time while my teachers and some of my friends, the other twenty percent, were on the other trying to whisper positive words into my head. The unfortunate part was that Gene's higher percentage outweighed those who were striving to lift me up even though he wasn't always directing his words at me.

With the days winding down to the show, my friends decided to suddenly turn the juggling act into a comedy routine where they started to juggle, and then as soon as someone messed up, the plan was for everyone to start throwing the juggling balls at one another like we were in a food fight. I was not up for that because if I was going to be in the talent show, I wanted to show my talent, not do something silly like that.

I saw this as my way out, and I didn't think twice. The day before the talent show, I decided I was not going to perform.

On the day of the talent show, I sat within earshot of Gene. All I could hear the entire time was Gene and his friends making fun of every performance.

"Look at 'em. So dumb. Idiots." He bent over laughing so hard but tried his hardest to keep the cackling from making any sound while little bursts of laughter jumped out between gasps for air.

His crew chimed in. "I know, right? They're so good. Not!"

Thank God I had stepped down from performing. That just confirmed I had made the right decision.

At the time, it felt like I had dodged a bullet, so to speak. But in retrospect, I realized I missed a truly unique opportunity to experience the joy of performing with friends in a talent show and replaced that joy with bitterness, regret, and guilt.

What I hadn't realized was I had given Gene even more power over me.

CHAPTER 3

In the private-school world, it was easy for parents to meet each other, network, and set up playdates. Fathers helped coach sports and parents organized carpools to get kids to and from practices and games.

I was in a carpool with almost every classmate at one time or another. But somehow, Gene and I were always in the car together. That meant more exposure to Gene's negative comments for thirty minutes after school.

"Art class sucked today. I hate that teacher. Can you believe she makes us do all that stuff? It's so dumb."

"Hmm," I let out a one-syllable laugh with my mouth closed because I was trying not to make him feel like I overly agreed with his statement. My wounded heart was weakening as I was indirectly targeted, because even though he was honed in on somebody else, I had a connection with that person. I couldn't find the courage to challenge him with, "Shut up. It's just because you suck at art."

He'd continue, "I don't see how you eat the cafeteria food. It's disgusting. I would never eat that trash. Yuck."

"Hmm," I mumbled again and turned away to try and escape the comments but knew there was nowhere to go. Through the glass window, the trees zoomed by one after the other and car horns honked in the rush hour traffic. I was searching for somewhere else to focus my internal thoughts and struggling to keep Gene's words out of my head. My chin sagged slightly, and now all I could see out the window was the wheel of the car next to us spinning so fast, just like my mind continuously recycling these daily comments.

Gene kept on. "Did you see how dumb Sam looked today with his socks pulled up so high? What an idiot." He cackled.

While trying to stay sitting straight up in the car seat, I stealthily stretched my arms toward my shins and slowly pushed my socks down closer to my ankles, hoping Gene had not seen mine. A warm sensation grew inside my chest as my thumping heart wanted to stand up, but my brain didn't allow it.

I resumed gazing out the window and thought about how I loved art class and how I semi-enjoyed the cafeteria food, but I was lost because I wasn't allowed to feel that way. My mouth stayed zipped on the account of my body freezing up out of fear for what Gene might say if I dared disagree with any of his statements.

One time he made a parent cry while she was driving us home because he made fun of someone's family who had just lost their mother in a car accident, and he was being very insensitive to the fact that adults in the community really cared about that lady. Real, genuine tears rolled down her face, and her bottom lip quivered.

"Stop!" she wailed. "How can you say those things? She was my friend!"

Gene turned red and put his tail between his legs before turning away and rolling his eyes. It was difficult to understand how he could say something so hurtful, but it made me feel even worse that I didn't have the strength to stand up and make him stop before she did. The rest of the car ride home, all one could hear was the sniffling, the short gasps for air, and the occasional click of the blinker.

At school, I couldn't seem to get away from him. Outside of school, it was just as bad. Because my parents had developed a strong friendship with his parents, we often hung out at his house as two families, and when it was time to leave, I ended up spending the night.

Gene used to give me his best sales pitch. "Hey, why don't you ask your parents if you can stay tonight? C'mon. We can keep playing games and stay up late."

"Okay, I'll check!" I exclaimed outwardly with a smile on my face, but inwardly, there was a part of me asking, "What are you doing?"

My problem was that I was afraid to say no because I feared what he would say about me if I didn't stay. However, if he was at my house and the same opportunity arose for him to spend the night at mine, he never did.

I'd say to Gene, "Hey, my parents said you can stay tonight if your parents say it's okay."

Despite doing the same activities at my house as we did at Gene's, he'd seem to fish for excuses. "My parents will say no. There's not much to do over here anyway."

Seriously? We had a television, video games, basketball hoop, and a swimming pool. I didn't understand. We even had a diving board, and he didn't.

During our middle-school ages, I probably spent the night at his house over a hundred times, but he spent the night zero times at mine. I knew it was because he was afraid to stay the night away from his parents, but because I had a genuine care and concern for putting other people's feelings before mine, I never made fun of him for it. I just let it go. His subtle, yet masterful way of using words to control others was not something I wished to bestow upon anyone else, not even Gene himself.

A typical day or evening over at Gene's house consisted of playing basketball outside in the driveway, playing video games, watching television or a movie, and lastly, swimming in the pool. That was what I considered the basic outline, but when you filled in the details, it was more like this . . .

We were out in the driveway shooting basketball having a grand old time. At times, I was in control as I cupped the rising ball in my palm and pushed it back toward the asphalt driveway creating a loud thud followed by a high-pitched ring. My life was like this basketball, though it was seemingly controlled by someone else. Its flexible membrane contorted and compressed ever so slightly against the ground but was never visible to the naked eye in fast motion.

Gene appeared as a professional athlete getting in his reps before the big game as he worked on his short game and layups, while I was heaving long distance shots like a cannon from as far away as I could. If I made one, Gene added, "Oh, you're so cool," in a sarcastic tone, and then he continued his layups and spin moves. After a while of his being annoyed by my shooting all the way from Mars, he wanted to prove he was better at basketball than me.

"Let's play one-on-one. Are you ready to lose? Again?" Gene challenged with his sly and scheming grin.

I shrugged, raised my eyebrows, and created a half smile as I tried not to roll my eyes.

I never wanted to compete. I wasn't sure how to explain it, but I just didn't care as much as he did about winning. Despite this fact, I reluctantly met the request and played one-on-one most of the time. And who do you think ordinarily won? Gene, of course.

Since he believed we were competing in a professional tournament against one another, he quickly did a spin move around me and laid it up. He announced the score and said, "Make it, take it!" Whenever I got a rebound on one of his misses, I dribbled the ball back out past the free-throw line, which was the rule, and before he could block my attempt, I shot it because I wasn't a good dribbler. Often, after I missed the shot, he corralled the rebound, quickly bolted out to the free-throw line, and then back to lay it up before I even recovered from where I had shot the ball, which was from outer space, remember? I never wanted to challenge the beast head-on because the obstacle ahead of me created a fear of what might happen if I conquered him. Therefore, I launched overhead instead of continuing my dribble and driving right through to the basket. I averaged about two baskets each time we played, and Gene sank about twenty. He was always happy because he had increased his devious control. It was one of the few times where he hadn't done the talking to gain power, instead using the game to best me.

When we finished playing basketball, we always went inside and got a drink. If I drank Coke too often and he drank water, I got made fun of for that.

"Wow. That's all you ever drink, isn't it?" He shook his head like I was an idiot.

It was too late now because I was already halfway through guzzling my sugar-filled beverage. Plus, I didn't respond.

We always watched movies and played video games.

"Hey, you wanna play the snowboard game again or watch a movie?" Gene asked.

"Hmm, I'm beat from all the basketball outside. I say let's watch a movie," I requested.

"No, let's play video games. C'mon, don't be like that. You

know it'll be fun."

Why did you even ask me if you don't care what I have to say?
The little voice inside me constantly responded in this way, but
my actual voice uttered, "Okay."

Video games went the same as basketball. I only wanted to
play racing games, and he only wanted to play shooting games,
at which I was horrible. So it was just another good two hours
of Gene beating me, and to make things worse, he made comments such as, "Dude. C'mon. I'm gonna have to play against
the computer next because you suck at this."

Later, if we were watching television with his parents, for
some reason, the whole time consisted of making fun of somebody on the screen.

"This is the worst movie ever. Switch it now," Gene demanded.

After a couple clicks, "Oh, let's see what's on the news real
quick," said Gene's parents.

Gene chimed in quickly, "Oh my gosh. This lady is so annoying. Just listen to her voice. Hands down, the worst news
reporter ever."

To my surprise, Gene's parents ignored these types of comments. Even worse, at times, they joined in even if it was a
simple, "I know, right?"

I just never understood it. I was always sitting there thinking,
Do y'all care about anything else besides critiquing everyone?

Then I'd catch myself during a funny commercial about to fall
off the couch from laughing so hard. "Oh my gosh!"

Gene shook his head. "Wow. Are you serious? That's not even
funny. So dumb."

Oh, right. What was I thinking? Those thoughts were never

mentioned out loud, but they were internal as my body turned warm from embarrassment. My personal choice to enjoy something on a television screen resulted in an anxious, tingling sensation inside my chest. *Why am I not allowed to laugh at that commercial if I think it's funny?*

I was straddling two completely different worlds. When I was not around Gene, I rarely heard negative comments about others. My parents didn't do it. My other friends didn't do it. Only Gene did it, but I was around him so much that it was like I was always traveling back and forth between these two different worlds and observing these opposite behaviors. All of these events were happening so subtly that nobody else except for me really even wondered if Gene was a bully. Little did he know I was taking in every word and analyzing it, even though I knew I should have been responding by saying my true thoughts.

To make things worse, when I was at school, I had an additional battle of trying to figure out where I fit best: the popular or unpopular crowd.

Gene's group was filled with sports, girls, and loads of laughter, yet the hysterics typically came at the expense of others.

At recess, most boys made their way to the soccer field. It was completely dry and barely growing with patches of dirt. The cute girls huddled near the set of bleachers to act like they weren't going to watch, but they sat there peering over their shoulders, smiling and giggling. Who knew which boy they were sipping tea over.

Gene smacked the ball out of another boy's hands and laughed as a cloud of dust began to rise. "Gimme the ball!" He smiled. "I'm captain. I pick . . ."

Gene's buddy, Crews, smirked and unsuccessfully tried to snatch the ball back from Gene. "Ha! Nice pick. Not! I'm the other captain. I'll take . . ."

I noticed how they all fired back at each other, and this was the norm, but I didn't fit that mold.

As the game ensued—"Center it! I'm open!"—another popular follower, Jackson, called for Gene to pass him the ball.

Once Gene created a clear path after juking around someone, he cocked his foot back as if he were about to send it right to him, but then he forcefully planted his front foot and lasered a shot at the goal as it went sailing over the crossbar.

"Dude! I was wide open! What are you doing? Pass the ball!" Jackson roared.

"But you suck! I could've passed it to your mom for a better shot than you would've taken."

"Very funny. Shut up, Gene. Just gimme the ball next time I'm open."

"Okay. Maybe. Not." He grinned.

What appeared as real arguments always turned into moments of "just kidding" or joking. This type of communication baffled me. Viewing the popular group from the outside appeared as though boys were taking genuine jabs at one another, but then it always got brushed over with a laugh and maybe a "you suck." You had to acquire this skill to officially initiate yourself into a part of this group, which was truthfully growing at a high rate.

Realistically, I fell into the unpopular group. Those people were my real friends, and they knew the real me, my real thoughts and feelings, and many of us felt the same about Gene and his people. Gene was out there converting all the popular kids to follow him.

"Hey, Tyler! Wanna come jump off the swings with us?" Sammie, one of my real friends, shouted.

I ran over, grabbed the swaying metal chains before they stopped. I plopped onto that yellow rubber seat, dug my toes into the gravel, and pushed myself backward on an upward slope. With every pump of my legs, my smile grew as I reached the highest point and could see the whole playground area, the soccer field, and everyone at recess.

"Tyler! Watch this!" Another true friend, Oliver, was swinging in sync with me. The wind blew the back of our hair forward, and in slow motion, as we reached the pinnacle of the backswing. "One!" We froze at the top. "Two!" Then like a car speeding downhill we reached the bottom. "Three!" He let go, flying high into the air like a bird until he landed not-so-gracefully, creating a small crater in the gravel with his shoes.

Oliver turned around, still hunched over, smiling. "That was awesome!"

"Look out below!" I launched myself off of the swing, landing with my feet first and then catching the rest of myself as my hands dug into the small pebbles.

"Tyler! Sweet!" Oliver cheered. He hadn't noticed I soared five feet past him. It wasn't a contest to him. Simply enjoying my company meant more to him as well as to the rest of my unpopular friends.

We all continued at our own pace, jumping off the swings, not caring who marked the furthest spot. Occasionally, when the timing worked, we let go at the same time and flew like a flock of birds. We instinctively understood one another, and that meant the world to me.

Unfortunately, I often struggled hanging with my not-so-popular friends and risking being made fun of by Gene and company. So I tended to make my way over to the popular crowd for safety. For example, if I spent fifteen minutes with the unpopular kids on the swings at recess, I then went and spent twenty to twenty-five minutes with the popular kids playing soccer or football. If I spent too much time with Gene's group, then the unpopular kids got frustrated with me. They didn't make fun of me, but they simply wished I didn't do that because they knew I hated how the popular kids operated. I was growing into something I didn't like, and that was being a fake person. It was disingenuous, and I felt guilty because my actions were not my true personality. Something needed to change soon if I was going to start living my best life.

CHAPTER 4

When kids begin fifth or sixth grade, they start to become more involved in sports. Since Gene was already so serious about winning so often, that just meant his competitive nature rose to a new level.

When we were growing up, I participated in almost every sport, which helped me develop basic techniques while also strengthening my hand-eye coordination. Often I fine-tuned my craft in each sport by practicing at home.

"Dad, will you play catch with me in the front yard?"

"Of course! Let me get my glove!"

My pops stayed out there for at least an hour, hunched over like a catcher, ready for every fastball I threw his way.

"Striiiiiike!" he belted and tossed the ball back to me. "Nice one!"

Over and over and over again, the repetition was helping my muscle memory to evolve so I could experience success.

For some reason, my hands and feet were always disproportionally larger than the size of my body, sort of like a big, clumsy puppy, except I was actually coordinated. Due to my extra-long eagle-like claws, I discovered I could grip the football well enough to launch it further than everybody in my grade level at school, and since many of the others knew this, even the popular kids requested for me to be the quarterback during recess time. I was okay with this because there was a three-Mississippi rule, which meant no one could rush the quarterback until after the count of three.

My favorite part, though, was the players on my team continued to run while the other team stopped running after a certain distance because they thought I couldn't throw it further than that, and then my teammate was usually there to catch the ball as it went sailing over the opposing team's heads as their jaws dropped to the ground. This was a skill that was discovered as young as second grade and was something that gave me popularity on the playground through to my middle-school years. *Thank you, Dad, for spending all those hours to help me develop my throwing motion.*

However, when it came to real football and tackling, I was scared straight. At recess, I never liked tackling anybody, and I never got tackled because I always released the ball before I got hit.

Sometimes when Gene had more than one friend over, they often wanted to play tackle football in the front yard, but I never truly wanted to do it. Occasionally I gave in for as long as I could, but I was a chicken looking for my way out. I told everyone I was just going to shoot hoops while they played. Basketball was always my cover.

At this age level, fifth and sixth graders played together on one football team, and seventh and eighth graders on another. As a fifth grader, of course I hadn't played because the sixth graders looked like the Hulk compared to me.

During lunch the day after a game, Gene and his friends chewed over the details of the battle. "Dude. Remember when we threw that prayer up on the last play of the half and actually scored? It was incredible!"

"That was awesome!" another chimed in.

"Do y'all know if Benny is okay though? I heard he broke his leg when he got sacked."

Wait a minute, so who's going to be the quarterback now?

The next time Benny showed up to school, it was confirmed: he had broken his leg while playing in the game. This just solidified my thinking. I should never play football. And because I hadn't participated, I was always left out of conversations about things that had happened at practice or games. Hearing about the fun moments and victories created an itch to partake in those moments together. Whenever we played at recess, friends still wanted me to be the quarterback, and I always heard how I should play for the school team, and it built up my confidence because I was wanted. Yet deep down, I was scared.

You know how the comments can be in middle school though. "Oh, c'mon. You're not scared to play for real, are you?" or "Nobody can throw the ball like you can." Oh, geez. That was supposed to make me feel so much better.

The fifth-grade year quickly passed, and as summer came to an end, it was time for football tryouts. Since Gene was so good at controlling my mind and my decisions, he did a great job of convincing me if I played this next year, it was going to be awesome. He talked about how I could be the quarterback, he would be the running back, and we would be unstoppable!

I had already felt so bad about not playing in fifth grade, but I tried to convince myself that when I was a sixth grader, and I would be older than the fifth graders on the team, so then I wouldn't have to worry so much about getting hit by someone younger and smaller than me.

I wanted to be a part of the group. They were beginning to really take over the grade level, and being part of the unpopular crowd was not cool. I wanted to be accepted. I felt like football was my chance to be popular.

The last thing Gene did to convince me to play, when he could tell I was hesitant, was tell me the first entire week of tryouts was not even in pads. There would be no hitting or tackling. Oh boy, I was in when he said that!

That first week of football was a dream. I was doing everything everyone else was, and I was accepted as a man because I was playing football. (Insert grunt.)

Everything was great because we were working as a team, and we were surviving the heat together. I wasn't getting hit, and life was amazing. The gigantic former-football-player-coaches made me feel good about myself. Then, after practice, I spent the night once or twice at Gene's where he further instilled in my mind this was the right choice because I was an awesome quarterback.

Sometime within that first week of football tryouts, school had started, and one crucial piece of information had not been relayed to me. Or more accurately, I had not done my research; instead, I relied on a con man to instill his truths into my pliable mind. Before I tell you that critical piece of information, I have to come clean. I was a chunky sixth grader. To put things into perspective, when my mom took me to the school uniform store, she requested husky-sized pants and shorts for me. No lie.

Now, let's get back to the missing piece of information Gene had never told me, which was the football team had a weight limit. What that meant was if you exceeded the weight limit set for the age group, they then put a huge red mark on the back of your helmet, and you could not be an offensive player that touched the ball. *Um, hello? Then how in the world am I supposed to be the quarterback?* So that meant I couldn't be the quarterback, or a running back, or a wide receiver, or anything except a lineman.

So what was the weight limit, and how much did I weigh? On the fifth and sixth grade team, the weight limit was set at 110 pounds. Most of the boys in the sixth grade weighed around eighty or ninety-something pounds.

I weighed a whopping 116 pounds!

Well, despite hearing this information, I felt like they would make an exception, and I didn't want to give up on having become a part of the cool group through football. It felt good to hear the positive comments Gene and others said about how well I could throw the ball, and I didn't want to lose that feeling.

Fast forward to week two of tryouts. Monday was the first practice with pads. Just putting them on made me feel even that much cooler. We did our typical warm up. I was feeling great. We got split up into small groups. Then we jumped into our first drill.

I was placed in the same group as Gene and a couple other "friends." They were really Gene's friends. I hadn't considered people who acted like him as my real friends. We were at the running-back station doing a drill where the coach had two players across from one another facing each other. One of those players was handed the ball by the coach, and the other player tried to tackle the runner. On the other hand, the running back was attempting to get around the defensive player without being taken down.

Let me just clarify this was only about two minutes into the real first practice with pads, minus the time we took for warming up.

Gene went as the first offensive player, and who do you think was the first defensive player? Me. How ironic. The coach blew his whistle and handed off the ball to Gene. I stepped toward him as he did a little shimmy with his shoulders along with a true spin move, and as I reached my arms out to attempt to wrap him up, he soared on by me like I was nothing. Boom—I ended up on the ground. The coach approved of Gene's performance. "Attaboy, son. Great footwork." To me, it was just another scenario of Gene on his high horse and me down in the dumps.

Now it was my turn to be the running back, but Gene had rotated to the back of the line, and I was to face off against a boy named Kevin. This boy had been the center the past season, and he was pretty good. I had high hopes I could get by him.

The coach blew the whistle and handed me the ball. I was so smart I decided to do the exact same 360-degree spin move Gene had done to the exact same side. Now let's imagine this in slow motion. I took one or two steps toward Kevin, my right shoulder started to turn backward as I began my spin move. My eyes slowly started to lose view of Kevin as I progressed 180 degrees into my turn.

Now fast forward... BAM!

As soon as my back was turned, he wrapped both of his arms around me and began to drive me the direction my face was looking, and he drove me down so hard onto the ground that I didn't just hit the ground. I had been hit with such great force that I was looking straight down into the dirt, through my facemask, while my legs and feet were straight up in the air before coming back down and hitting the ground. My body was contorted like a scorpion.

I don't even remember the rest of practice. All I could think about was how that hit sent me into oblivion, and I did not ever want it to happen again. So how was I going to make that happen? By quitting. As soon as I saw my parents after practice, I told them I did not want to continue. I wasn't going to tell people I was too afraid of being hit like that again, so my main excuse was I was not going to be the quarterback anyhow because I was not under the weight limit.

The following days at school were the worst. My main memory is of girls asking me why I had quit football and was it because I was too scared? There was nothing worse than a girl thinking I wasn't brave. I lived in my own little mental bubble of horribleness about the whole thing. I never stepped foot back onto the football field. It was a really difficult decision—one I made on my own without input from anyone. I lived with that personal choice and all the backlash from curious classmates. That fall season was rough, but on the horizon was baseball.

CHAPTER 5

To this day, my sister claims out of all the sports I ever played growing up, and I played almost all of them, I was the best at baseball. If I was supposed to be the quarterback in football, which position do you think I played most in baseball? Pitcher.

I started baseball very young. First with T-ball, then I progressed to coach pitch, followed by machine pitch, and lastly, kid pitch.

In the very early stages of my baseball life, I could throw a baseball further than I could a football, and not only that, I was pretty good at hitting. Why was I good at hitting? Because the ball was either sitting still on a tee, a trustworthy dad was slowly tossing the ball to me, or a decently fast machine was throwing the ball to the exact same location every single pitch. I never had anything to worry about... until kid pitch.

Honestly, I really enjoyed it at first because I was the pitcher, and I threw the ball harder than most. So whenever it was my turn to go up to bat, the opposing pitcher didn't throw the ball as hard as me, so I wasn't scared, and since that was the case, I crushed the ball.

I was pretty sure the year was the same one when I had quit football. And I knew if I did the same with baseball in the middle of a season that same year, my life as I knew it would have been over.

"Oh, Tyler. Why did you quit baseball?" I could already hear the girls asking me. There was no way I was going to let it come to this.

As sixth grade continued, it was very apparent my teammates were growing, getting stronger and taller. Everyone was becoming better athletes. I still enjoyed playing baseball because I was getting even better at pitching. But it was this particular year in which all of the pitchers in the league began throwing the ball fast. No, I did not say they were throwing strikes. What I meant was, they were throwing it as hard as they could with hopes the ball went over the plate. It was wild pitch after wild pitch, keeping you on your toes. Was it going to go over the catcher's head and hit the back fence behind him? Was it going to go straight into the dirt before reaching home plate? Was it going to be a crazy, wild pitch outside that the catcher couldn't even lunge for? Or was it going to be the big kahuna laser, directly at… me?!

I remembered one specific game that stuck out in my mind. I was pretty sure I had already been hit, maybe just once while batting that year, but at this game, something interesting happened.

There was a left-handed pitcher who obviously wanted to make a name for himself, but honest-to-goodness, he just wasn't a good pitcher. He looked cool. He played the part. But he couldn't throw the ball straight!

Here's a play-by-play in the moment. The crowd hushed except for a few parents yelling encouragement. "You got this! Wait for the right one! If it ain't your pitch, then it ain't your pitch! Take it to 'em!"

Gene was up at bat. He settled into his stance. The pitcher wound up for a fast one and let it fly. Whack! Gene got hit by a fast pitch, and he was hurt badly. He walked to first base, wincing and fighting back tears as our next batter approached the plate. Here came the first pitch . . . and... BAM! Kid number two got hit just like Gene! Moms and dads in the stands got a little upset now—players were getting nervous. Our third batter reluctantly approached the plate. I'll let you guess . . .

Yes! You are correct! He got hit by the pitch, and then the pitcher started hearing it from the players on our team, but not me though because I'm nonconfrontational. "Take him out!" "He needs to be ejected!" "He can't pitch!" And Gene was over there saying, "He sucks! Take him out!"

Anyway, all I could think about at this moment was *I'm going to be next!* Honestly, what were the odds he would actually hit me now? With all those raging fans in the stands, and all the angry players on the field? Wouldn't he try his honest-to-goodness best to throw the ball over the plate?

The umpires and coaches calmed everyone down, and they kept "Mr. Wild Pitch" in the game.

I think the first pitch came, and I cringed a little bit thinking it was going to come straight at me, but it zoomed on by, and the umpire yelled, "Striiiiiiiike!" I thought, *Wow, of course that happened.* I also thought, *Okay, he has gained his control back.*

Pitch number two. Here it came. The pitcher eyed down home

plate, went into his throwing motion, released the ball along with a loud grunt, and as the ball began spinning toward the plate, I took notice it was not going to go over the plate this time, but rather, here it came again, right at the batter, and that batter was me!

I had no time to duck or get out of the way, so I just turned my back to the ball, and BAM! All the red stitching dug right into my back. I don't remember the rest of the game. All I knew was another mental battle was about to ensue.

After that, every time I went up to bat, no matter what game it was, I thought I was going to get pummeled. I thought this because I had gone up thinking I wasn't going to get hit, but I had. I think the other players and coaches on my team simply thought I wasn't playing as well, and I was in a slump.

After that one incident, I always went up to bat and swung at all three pitches just to get out. I was shaking in my shoes. The memory of being hit, and the pain that followed, was so great I couldn't overcome it.

I had no desire to get hit by anything. Not by a person. Not by a ball. I just wasn't your typical boy that liked to horseplay rough with his friends. I didn't want to invade other people's space, so I wasn't going to enjoy that with anybody because I didn't want others crossing the threshold of my own invisible bubble that surrounded me.

So since I knew there was no way I could quit baseball too, I had to finish out the season, which I did. I rarely got on base from all the free swinging I was doing. All I knew was if I made it through the season, then nobody could say I quit baseball. If I didn't play in seventh grade the following year, then I wasn't quitting if I didn't play to begin with, and that was my plan.

I never played baseball again. How depressing. No more football, no more baseball, no more . . . who knew? The fear of getting hurt was just too great for me to continue with any of these sports. Now I have no idea if I could have been a great quarterback or a great pitcher. But I do know this: quitting both sports gave me a way to distance myself from Gene even more.

But when would I find something where I wouldn't throw in the towel or hang up my cleats for good?

CHAPTER 6

I n the midst of quitting football and baseball, the verbal bullying felt more intense. It wasn't that the comments were
being aimed in my direction, but they were being sprayed in
all directions, and I always heard them.

Think about when you have heard a bully, and how they have
done the majority of their work indirectly. For example, they've
talked about others behind their backs instead of to their faces.
In fact, you knew they were talking about you when they looked
your way and started to laugh.

Everyone was gathered around the cafeteria table. Gene muttered, "Guys, look at Kevin. I know he's good at football, but he's
such a pig." Kevin was still in line getting his food.

"Oh my gosh. Check it out. A double helping of beans," Crews
added.

Oink, oink! The pig snorts made their way around the table,
and all were cackling except for me. I was always wondering
why? What was the purpose of judging and analyzing Kevin in
such a way? I thought he was considered one of their friends,
and he was.

Then he finally made his way to the table with his tray overflowing.

Jackson welcomed him. "Kevin! Hey, big guy!" Some were trying to hold back but still spurting out bursts of spit through their closed lips, like squeezing a sports water bottle. Only Kevin had to ponder what all the silliness was about, but then Gene mischievously changed the topic—"You ready for the big game this week?"—the newly formed football conversation quickly overshadowed the short stint of comments, and they all moved on as if nothing had ever been mentioned about Kevin.

There was a time when the verbal bullying really got to me. I was tired of things being said about others, and I hated being in and out of the different groups. I wanted to be left alone, and I wanted no part in the nonsense. I had no desire to be a typical middle-school boy who horsed around and played jokes on others.

One day we were in social studies class, which was in the very last classroom on the left at the end of the hallway. We were working independently on an assignment that was very craft-materials-based. Basically we needed glue, scissors, and paper. The teacher was wrapped up with a situation occurring somewhere else within the school, so her mind wasn't focused on paying attention to any of us.

The popular boys were doing their typical thing on the other side of the room: making fun of others, laughing, and messing with people.

Crews was squeezing dabs of glue onto his fingertips and touching the other boys' papers. "Oops!" he snickered. "I'm so sorry!"

"Oh yeah?" Jackson picked up his assignment and rubbed the glob of glue on Crews's forearm. "How about that?"

Another boy joined in. "Yours sucks anyway, Jackson, so I'm just fixing it with a little extra glob." He ripped the paper out of Jackson's hands and proceeded to squeeze a tiny puddle of glue right into the center.

Crews erupted in laughter along with the other boy. "Oh my gosh! Look at it!"

Then, to my utter bewilderment, Jackson responded with a wide-mouthed smile and both his hands covering his mouth and nose.

The entire popular group couldn't stop laughing about the whole scenario. Yet again, I was baffled how they went from picking on each other to brushing it off as nothing.

After a short break from playing with the glue, they realized, "Hey, we have scissors! We could probably do something really stupid with these!"

The teacher had actually ended up leaving the room to handle the other ongoing situation and asked us to continue independently. Ha. We should have been silently working, but all you could hear were the boys snickering about what they were plotting to do with their newfound toys.

"Dude, she left the room," Crews whispered.

"Are you thinking what I'm thinking?" Jackson looked out of the corner of his eye and half smiled.

As usual, someone provided additional commentary. "This assignment is so dumb. Can you believe she left us in here? All she does is give us stuff to do and never teaches anything."

I was already so angry from hearing all the comments and they were becoming less filtered with every passing second. I wasn't mad from this one moment. I had grown infuriated from all of the previous years building up, and things had seemed to be getting worse when one might think people would mature with age.

"Some people here could use a bit of help with their style, you know what I mean?" Jackson mumbled under his breath, except he was louder than most, so it flowed crystal clear into my ears.

"Yeah, I know, right?" Crews chuckled.

The wolf pack was now huddled in and rustling about who knows what.

One interesting fact about this whole scenario was that Gene was not even present in this particular class with us, but even though he was in a different classroom that period, years of his unending influence were seeping through the walls into my classroom. It was like he was in there.

I had been facing away from the group of boys, and I grew quieter and quieter as my discontent kept building. I was like a teakettle on the stove heating up. I was no longer talking to anybody at my table. I was in a zone of frustration with steam coming out of my ears and nose.

Then I heard whispers about cutting someone's hair with the scissors. Then there was chuckling. And finally, the faint whispers.

Suddenly I knew an innocent student in the classroom had been selected to be preyed upon, but I didn't know yet which victim was the chosen one. The perpetrator was never somebody like Gene. Anyone who had acquired Gene-like wit was too smart to actually be the one to do something with the scissors, but anyone like him was the perfect person to mastermind the plan and hatch it without being identified. Despite his absence,

Gene was still the one pulling the strings because his impact and popularity reached so far. It was like he was somewhere else sitting at his master control panel pushing all the buttons to create what was about to happen. There was no telling who would be the one to attempt something so absurd.

As I continued working and listening intently, I could hear the footsteps and soft laughs moving around the room. Those steps and laughs seemed to be getting closer to the back of my chair. Then I could feel whoever it was standing right behind me as you could hear Gene's posse at their table, laughing and saying, "Do it . . ."

Do what? Actually cut my hair? I stayed facing away and continued working and looking only at my work, still not completely sure if it was me who had been chosen.

Then I felt the fingers touch the back of my head. I truly believed there was no way this boy was going to do something like this, and if he did, what was I even going to do about it?

The encouragement from the boys became stronger. "Do it... c'mon... do it."

SNIP!

POP!

The scissors sliced right through my hair, and I saw some of it fall down like feathers over my shoulders, and just as fast as the scissors chopped my locks, I stood, and all in one single 180-degree motion, I punched the boy right in the face. The room fell silent.

As my heart was pounding through my chest, my first thought was *Oh... my... God. What have I done?!* It was Crews! My anxiety heightened because I knew if he chose to fight back, I was toast. However, he didn't. He rubbed his face where I hit him and moaned about it while he walked back to his desk. I immediately sat back down and continued working while I wondered what my punishment would be.

Seconds later, the teacher walked back into the room.

Keep in mind, in private middle school, telling on one another was very common. Everyone did it. And people under Gene's wings knew so well how to play the victim card even though it was all those within their pathway who were the true victims.

Yet on this particular day, after this isolated series of events, a surprising thing happened that, to this day, I've never witnessed again. Not a single soul said anything to the teacher—ever—about what happened in class that day.

This held true despite the fact that Crews had a huge red mark on the side of his face, welling up in a large area. You could have even seen the ruby red blossom swell the following class period. No students that witnessed the punch ever said anything about it, and no teachers who ever saw Crews's face suspected it was from my capable fist.

The only logical reasoning for this turn of events was this: No one could believe that I, me, this kid, the one who couldn't hurt a fly, had actually done something so violent, so headstrong, so thoughtless to another human being.

Even today, years after the event, I wish the journey had ended without the punch, but even so, their actions didn't change.

CHAPTER 7

---

hroughout all these agonizing years, I found it more and more difficult to retreat from what appeared to be a friendship with Gene. Not only that, but I was still spending the night often and hanging out with him on the weekends. My parents were still best friends with his parents, and the years kept adding up. It was like eating the most savory sweets and enticing junk food daily without understanding time was ticking, and the poor choice to allow myself to continue was putting an extra weight on my shoulders I couldn't carry. Not only that, but the plaque of life was building up on my brain, and nobody was aware of the contamination taking place. People have consumed harmful foods while knowing they were hurting themselves, and for many of them, the temptation was stronger than the thought of the long-term consequences; but for me, the overpowering factor was fear, and it was affecting my logical decision-making to retreat because of everything happening with Gene. When adding up all the wasted years as his friend, I could finally begin to understand how much of a mental toll this kind of abuse was having on me.

How many years had it been so far? I met Gene in kindergarten, and we were now entering the seventh grade, so I had officially spent seven full years in his presence under his authoritarian rule.

As I grew older, I learned people tended to behave based on the environment in which they were surrounded. For example, if the majority of students in a class were hardworking and attentive, then even the kids who behaved poorly acted better because the majority were being good.

Everyone knew to never test the science teacher, Mr. Reagan. He was a bit heavier with his two-sizes-too-small polo tucked in and his belly hanging over the edge covering his belt. His shiny, slick black hair matched his thick-rimmed glasses. Even as he sat in his chair across the room, he struck fear in most. "Class, I need everyone seated, all voices off, and eyes up front."

We all stayed put. Then Jackson casually waltzed over to Mr. Reagan at his desk and stood frozen staring straight ahead.

Mr. Reagan took off his glasses and squinted. "Excuse me, son. I believe I said voices off and eyes up front. What part of this do you not understand?"

Jackson was trying not to smile. To all the students, it was obvious now what he was doing. Not only had he powered off his voice, but his eyes were now physically located inside his head at the front of the room. However, even though the majority had the itch to snicker, we all held back.

Then it clicked for Mr. Reagan too. "Jackson, since you love the extra attention, I need your voice off and your eyes right here after school."

"But Mr. Reagan, I was just—"

"You will be cleaning the entire lab. I will notify your mother."

It was moments like these where we learned not to be the minority in the room who chose to act out.

Sometimes I wished I had guts like Jackson or Gene to take risks and step out of my comfort zone, but when I had a live shot of the potential negative consequences, whether it was in class or socializing with friends, I chose to remain comfortable. Deep down, though, when it came to overcoming the mental battles with Gene, I sensed I needed to channel my inner beast mode in order to conquer my fears.

But what if there were repercussions for my choices and actions? Those feelings paralyzed me from making a change that could ultimately benefit my life. The old saying, be careful what you wish for—getting that freedom could bring a list of unintended consequences scarier than staying put. My phobia of what might happen if I tried to escape the confines of Gene's control overshadowed my visions of achieving the ultimate freedom I desperately desired.

I grew up in the Michael Jordan era, and the one boy at our school who was the best at any sport he played was named Micah. This boy's dad had even played competitive college basketball at some point, and Micah was mainly known for not joining in our other team sports growing up because, even as a first grader, he was already traveling and playing for select soccer teams.

When we were at recess playing soccer, it was always, "I'm on Micah's team!" However, Micah was pretty much his own team. He could keep the ball away from every person on the field for all of recess if he wanted to. He was so good at handling the ball and making people miss when they lunged for it. It was like catching a fly; you always thought you got it, but after every swing and swipe, you'd come up short.

Micah could stand there with his foot perched atop the ball, daring me to try and steal it. "Go ahead. You have plenty of time. I'm just standing here." He shrugged his shoulders and yawned.

Feeling like I had turned the rocket boosters on behind my shoes without his noticing, my leg stretched forward at Mach speed. He effortlessly rolled the ball backward out of the pathway of my swing so that I almost fell over as the weight of my foot continued forward. Our brains couldn't match the speed of his decision-making. He somehow knew when to tap it left, tap it right, pop it around one side of me, through my legs, or over my head and race on by, sprinting toward the goal. The same tape played on repeat for everyone most of recess. I wasn't the only one making an attempt to dethrone the king of sports.

All the girls loved Micah and wanted to be with him, and all the boys wanted to be him.

Before seventh grade, Micah wouldn't even play on our non-school basketball team in the recreational league because he was off playing true competitive basketball like he had done with soccer.

In our school, once you were in seventh grade, it was time to get serious about sports, especially basketball, because this was the first time we experienced having a real tryout. Not only were some at a disadvantage due to Micah's natural abilities, but he had grown to a monstrous six feet four inches in our seventh-grade year. I didn't sprout quite as high, but my cheek bones started to become more visible, and even my middle-school love handles weren't there to hold onto anymore.

Basketball tryouts were considered real tryouts, not because anyone was going to be cut from the team, but because there were going to be some boys put on the A Team and the remaining losers on the B Team. Basketball was different than football or baseball for me because I loved shooting the ball.

All those hours in my driveway, I placed my left hand on the side for support and my right hand underneath with my elbows bent and my feet and shoulders squared up to the basket. I pushed off the ground with my toes and slowly stretched toward the sky as I snapped my right wrist forward toward the hoop with the small bumps of the ball rolling off of my fingertips, creating a smooth backspin, and more often than not, SWOOSH! It passed through the center of the net, pulling it down like a rubber band before splashing back up higher than the rim until gravity let it fall back into place.

Not only did I favor basketball because of this, but also, I couldn't get hit quite like I could in the other sports I had tried. This was my chance to become part of the popular group again. Everyone knew I could shoot. I just couldn't dribble, and I didn't want to either.

I had attended many basketball camps with Gene during various summers, and he was always way more competitive than me. Now we were in a very high-strung environment: middle-school basketball tryouts. I began to mentally count who would probably be on the A Team before we even began: Gene, Micah, Crews, Jackson, and all the same boys I considered to be a part of Gene's crew. They were all so ruthless, so judgmental, and so opinionated. I always thought to myself, "Why do y'all care so much?" I knew I deserved to be on the A Team, but I simply just didn't want to be.

I also began to think, "Hey, there is an A Team and a B Team, and whichever one I make, I am going to be spending a lot of time around those people." I began to realize this was a way to get away from Gene and a great opportunity to slide under the radar and spend less time with him.

Even though I knew I was going to miss out on an opportunity to play with the one and only Micah, I was more focused on self-preservation. You know what I did for the remainder of tryouts? I missed as many shots as I could on purpose.

One might think I wasn't good enough to be on the A Team. However, in this same year, I entered a free-throw shooting contest and won at the school level. Then I won within the district. After that, I almost won at the city and barely missed out on a chance to go to the state level. Therefore, I was good enough for the A Team.

However, I truly didn't try for the duration of tryouts, and when the rosters were posted a few days later, I zoomed in to see the piece of paper pinned to the bulletin board in the crowded hallway, a heavy weight instantly falling off of my shoulders. My plan worked! I was on the B Team! I forcefully hung my head low while everyone was nearby, but the hopes inside my heart were soaring. There probably had never been a kid in the history of middle school, or sports, as happy to be placed on the lesser team. Now I was no longer going to have to worry if I missed a shot or didn't perform well. There was no more added pressure from hearing all the negative comments. I was going to have the chance to play with the kids who were my real friends, like Sammie and Oliver.

The season was great that year in seventh grade. I got to play in the B League, and this might have seemed slightly criminal, but I was averaging twenty points per game.

I made three pointers. I made layups. I stole the ball. I blocked the ball. I felt like Michael Jordan. The best part though was no Gene.

Another perk? Gene always asked how well we had done, probably hoping we had lost each time.

"We won fairly easily, actually." I kept my poker face.

Gene was in disbelief. "Oh yeah? Did you even score at all?"

"I scored twenty-two points." I didn't tell him it was the highest on the team. "How did you guys do in your game?" My genuine heart hoped they had done well because we all knew how Gene handled things if I outperformed him.

"Well, you see, I didn't play because I rolled my ankle at practice the other day, and the coach wanted me to rest. Kevin had to fill in for me, and he sucked it up, so we lost." He huffed, shook his head, and rolled his eyes.

Again, with his magical manipulative words, he turned things around so that my success wasn't acknowledged, and his defeat was put on someone else.

On other occasions, he took the opportunity to let me know if they had won and conversely rubbed it in when we had lost. If I added in how many points I had scored, he then asked what our record was which might not have been great, so he followed that up by making sure I knew the A Team had more wins than losses.

Remember, even though I had won by making the B Team, I was still losing by being around Gene during class, lunch, recess, and outside of school. It never stopped. *How am I going to get away from this guy?* Even after all of my hard work to separate myself, a very small part of me pondered the old saying, if you can't beat 'em, join 'em.

CHAPTER 8

As the years flew by, my fear grew stronger. No matter what, I always had voices in my mind telling me what Gene thought about me because I always heard his opinions about others.

One example I always remember from this time was during our morning carpool. There were four boys who rode together: Gene, Micah, Sammie, and myself. On this particular day, Sammie was waiting outside of his home for us to arrive. He was the fourth and final boy to be picked up. When Gene saw him as we pulled up, he rolled his eyes. "Oh my God. I cannot believe he is wearing that stupid shirt again. I hate that shirt. Why does he always wear that?"

Seriously? I thought, but I never said it. One second later, Sammie got into the car, and Gene changed his demeanor and offered a welcoming, "Hey!"

It was these sorts of things that happened every single day, and that meant I heard them all the time. So when something like that happened as often as it did, you could imagine how paranoid all of us had become about who was next up to be criticized.

I knew for a fact he made fun of me one time for how often I wore my favorite football jersey, and you know what? I stopped wearing it if I knew I was going to see Gene.

Since my parents were very hard workers during the day, we usually ate out for dinner. One evening, we headed to a local Italian restaurant we liked to frequent on Tuesdays.

"Oh, I like that song," my sister announced. "Can you turn it up a little?"

I perked up, waiting for Mom to turn the dial to the right. From the passenger seat, she reached with her left hand and pinched the sides of the volume knob but immediately went all the way to the left.

"Mom!" Michelle shouted. "What are you doing?"

"Excuse me?" Mom responded ever so calmly. "We hardly ever get to see each other during the day. I want to hear all about your day at school."

Michelle groaned. "Mom . . ."

"Go ahead. I'm waiting."

Michelle proceeded, "Okay, so I went to school. I sat in a chair. I wrote on paper numerous times. I turned my work in to my teachers. And now I'm here. How was that? Can you turn the song back up now?"

Mom immediately turned over her left shoulder and gave Michelle 'the look' with her eyebrows raised and her head tilted slightly downward as if looking over invisible glasses on the edge of her nose. At the end of a long day, Mom didn't want to deal with it, so she reluctantly turned the volume back up only enough to hear the muffled beat through the speakers as she continued conversation with my dad. Michelle rolled her eyes and glared out the window with her arms crossed. I sat there, minding my own business, feeling every slight bump in the road.

I zoned out for a few minutes until I heard the clicking sound of the turn signal as we pulled into the parking lot of the restaurant.

"So, Tyler. How about you? Can you tell me about your day?" Mom asked.

And then I saw it. The bright red vehicle. It had to be theirs, but I wasn't totally sure. All I knew was seeing what I thought was Gene's parents' car caused my heart to immediately begin beating a mile a minute. Suddenly I remembered and grabbed my shirt to feel the material. Oh no! I was wearing my favorite blue mesh jersey I had worn a hundred times too many.

"Tyler? Hello?" Mom wondered where my head was.

My dad put the car in park. I took a big gulp, and with the repeated heavy thuds inside my chest, I responded, "I'll tell you when we get inside."

I put one foot in front of the other as slowly as I could, hoping it wasn't their car. The restaurant's mirror-tinted windows were heightening my insecurities as my reflection peered back at me.

We passed through the doorway. "Hello, good evening. How many will there be?"

I began scanning the entire area from where I was standing, but I couldn't see Gene or his family. Maybe it wasn't them. I should be okay.

"We have four," my dad responded.

"Follow me, please. Right this way."

We followed the hostess through the maze of tables and seating areas. The entire place was full of walls that jutted out into open space separating each little nook. She led us past the continual row of booths along the windows and took a sharp right turn around one wall. The whole time I kept wondering but was trying to think optimistically.

"Here you go. Your server will be with you shortly."

I breathed a huge sigh of relief, but before I could sit all the way down in my chair, a head peeked from around the next protruding wall. "Hey there!"

"Hey!" My mom stood out of her chair to give Gene's mom a hug. She waved her hand and motioned for us to come over.

I took a deep breath and tried to cross my arms over my jersey number to try and hide it as best as I could without looking rude. I kept my left arm frozen in place and quickly raised my right arm to give a courtesy wave and smile.

While our parents greeted one another, Gene looked at me grinning. He pointed at me but wasn't looking at my eyes. He gave a tug on his own shirt, shook his head, and laughed to himself. When his parents turned to see what he was snickering about, he swiftly spoke, "Hey, Tyler. What's up?"

"Hey, Gene." I nodded.

Their waitress barged in balancing the tray of fresh-plated food high in one hand and folding open the tray stand with the other. She carefully set everything down.

My dad jumped in. "Well, y'all don't let us keep you from your dinner. Enjoy."

I could still see Gene smirking as we settled back at our table.

I wasn't able to break through the mental wall I had created inside myself. Instead, it was like I was pounding my own head against it. I wished I didn't care so much, yet I was never more grateful than to have the physical wall there to block my view from Gene's deceitful gestures.

For self-preservation, I memorized Gene's parents' license plate number. We continually ran into them in public because we ate out for dinner so much. Whenever we pulled into any parking lot with a similar red vehicle, I speedily scanned the letters and numbers off the back plate to see if it was a match. When my internal computer confirmed the coast was clear, in a completely relaxed and confident manner, I got out of the car to enjoy time with my family. However, if my central processing unit declared there was a threat, I then begged my parents to go somewhere else, but they had no idea my motivation for leaving. I told them Gene was there at the restaurant, and they responded with a very confused "So . . .?" I think my sister understood me, but my parents probably wanted to see their friends, so we rarely changed our plans.

Similar to how my parents never retreated from a situation like this, I hardly ever declined anything suggested by the dictator himself. One day, on a half day of school, Gene decided to mastermind a prank on Sammie. He organized the other boys, myself included, to gaslight Sammie into thinking we were all going to Six Flags after school. The truth was, we weren't going anywhere.

Therefore, as we carpooled home, we were all acting excited about Six Flags.

"Have you guys heard about the new roller coaster that has three loops in it?" announced Micah.

"Dude. And I heard it brings you like six stories high into the air at the very beginning and drops you into oblivion," added Gene.

Sammie sat up straight. "I love roller coasters! My dad was going to bring me there for my birthday this year, but then it rained, so this will be great!"

"Sweet," Gene gave him a fist bump.

I feared being the one to mess things up, but my conscience was beginning to feel the guilt trip.

We decided after we all got dropped off at home, we would all change clothes and get ready, and then at a specified time, we would pick everyone back up, and a parent would take us to Six Flags. Fun, right? Wrong.

We were all there snickering, and then I later found out Sammie had made sure his parents knew about Six Flags, and they were fine with it as long as he locked the door of their house from the inside before he left because he didn't have a key. When he went outside to wait for the pickup at one o'clock, he was sitting outside on the curb unable to get back into his house for approximately two hours in the hot, blazing sun. He parked there with his hat and full water bottle, but once he drank it dry and stared at the ring of sweat on his favorite t-shirt, it hit him. Nobody was coming. Sammie spent the rest of the afternoon seeking shade and cooler temperatures on his front porch. The worst part about this was I couldn't believe I had participated in this terrible plot. Now Sammie's parents were upset, but they never assumed or learned I did something like this to their son. He was one of my best friends from the "unpopular" group, the B Team! Truthfully, I was devastated.

On the other hand, Gene and Micah, they couldn't stop laughing, and of course they declared it was "just an April Fool's joke."

After having the awful feeling from participating in this prank, I knew I did not want to help with anything like that ever again.

However, when the next prank occurred, things changed dramatically.

CHAPTER 9

Seventh grade was in the books. I had now officially logged eight full years of Gene's influence on my life. I had one more full year in eighth grade before high school, when I could potentially leave Gene for good, but before that could happen, I had to survive the summer first.

A typical summer consisted of many basketball camps with Gene and company. However, when this particular one began, I recalled we did not have the same schedule for the first week, which was unusual because I'm telling you, we usually did the same thing together until school resumed, unless it was a football camp, of course.

At the end of that first week, I remembered Gene, Micah, and Jackson saying how amazing tennis camp at the nearby Tennis Academy had been. They announced they were definitely doing it again, and I should sign up to join in on the fun.

Gene proclaimed, "I've never had more fun in one week. You have got to try it."

"Totally," Jackson gave a serious thumbs up.

Well, who says no to Gene? Not me. Not yet, anyhow. So I signed up. I was even more excited because the one and only Micah was attending, and remember, everyone wanted to be like Micah, including myself.

Sunday evening came, and I was getting antsy to attend tennis camp the next day with the boys. I had never played tennis before, and I thought it could be fun. Monday morning finally came. I woke up, got ready, and one of my parents dropped me off inside the tennis pro shop as I got introduced to the head teaching pro for the camp, Stacy, who was so bubbly and welcoming.

"Good morning! What a beautiful day for some tennis! How are you? What's your name?"

Shocked by the very warm greeting, I simply said, "Tyler."

Stacy wasn't fazed. "Tyler! Great! How perfect is that? Tyler starts with a T! Tennis starts with a T! We are going to have so much fun!"

I smiled and nodded.

Wanting to make sure I was taken care of, Stacy suggested, "Why don't you go find yourself a seat near the courts while we wait for everyone else to get here?"

It was about eight forty when I arrived, and camp was supposed to start at nine a.m. Gene and the other boys had not arrived yet, but there were a good number of kids showing up as we waited outside.

At this time in my life, I was thirteen years old. As I stood there watching the time tick closer to nine a.m., they still hadn't arrived. And as I looked around, I began to notice even though there were about twenty other kids there, the next oldest was about eight years old and was entering third grade the following year while I was entering eighth. I finally realized Gene and the others had not signed up for the camp.

Was I now the brunt of a joke? Anyhow, I was here at tennis camp, and there was no hiding. I even got a little extra one-on-one attention being the oldest, and that helped me learn more. As the week progressed, I was enjoying myself because tennis wasn't easy to grasp quickly, and I was determined to figure it out in the same way I had learned to juggle. I wanted to master the skill.

I frequently got home at the end of a full day of tennis camp out in the blistering sun, and I asked my dad to go hit with me at the public courts nearby, and even though he never played tennis, he graciously obliged because he saw my desire to get better. I was grateful he was willing to support me in moments like these no matter what sport or talent I was trying to obtain.

"Whoa! What a shot," my dad shouted. "You're not that bad. Speaking of bad . . ." He pointed to himself and laughed.

"Dad, you haven't ever played. I'm just glad you came to hit with me."

We only carried about six tennis balls with us, so once we emptied our pockets, it was time to pick them up and start over.

I bent over to get the last ball near the back fence, but instead of using my hand, I applied some of my new tennis skills and swung downward to bounce the strings on top of the stagnant ball, smushing it slightly toward the court and letting it slowly spring into the air with a few extra light wisps of the racquet until the ball rose high enough for me to catch it with my hand. The tennis ball flexed the same way the basketball did when I played in the driveway with Gene, but something was different.

There was something poetic about the smooth motion of swinging at a tennis ball and seeing the strings grab the fuzz to lift the ball past the net. This central barrier of the court was like the obstacle in my life I was trying to get over, yet this time, I controlled where the ball went because nobody was on my side of the court waving their arms or hands in my face trying to steal the victory from me.

"Here you go, Dad!" I took the tennis ball in my left hand then let it bounce off the asphalt court and back up into my strike zone. Thud! I sent my dad a slow courtesy shot so he could hit it back over, and when he did, my feet danced into the perfect position, and I bent my knees to load my legs with the weight in my toes. My shoulders did a quarter turn to the right, and my eyes honed in on the incoming ball. I subconsciously bit my bottom lip lightly, and once it got close enough, I uncoiled my torso to the left and pushed up and through the ball. The strings making contact let out a springing sound followed by a short pop and a fleeting echo. It was like music to my ears.

That week ended, and even though I had been tricked into signing up for tennis camp, I had enjoyed myself, and part of it was because Gene wasn't there. *Hey, I like tennis, and Gene hates it. If I sign up for tennis camp again, he probably won't. Then, if that happens, I won't have to be around him, and I can keep learning how to play!*

So guess what happened?

I signed up for the next six weeks in a row, which was the remainder of their camps for the summer. Gene only joined during one of those weeks. He thought tennis was stupid, and my skills had progressed enough that he wasn't better than me like he was at basketball, so he didn't want to be a part of tennis. My heart was content because he didn't like it.

There was another main reason I began to really enjoy myself. I had been in the beginner-level tennis camp, but as the weeks went by, I was really learning a lot. I was already athletic from all the other sports I had played, and it wasn't like I was sitting at home playing video games all day. I liked to run around and play sports.

What really opened my eyes to this new sport was there was a more advanced group of kids who practiced together each day. They were really good, but I wasn't quite there yet. The thing that stuck out to me though was they seemed to always be having so much fun together, and it was different from how Gene and his friends defined it. This kind wasn't because they were laughing together while making fun of somebody. It was far from that.

From a distance, I watched six of them practice drills on one court, although the entire group of kids consisted of many more on all the surrounding courts.

Stacy announced, "Alright! I'm feeding you one deep ball followed by one short ball. After you complete both, get back in line. If you hit one of these standing targets on my side, everyone else has to do ten push-ups each time." She had two empty tennis-ball baskets propped on one half of her side of the net for them to direct their shots. "Ball in! Let's go!" Slowly but surely, the sound of popcorn began to expand around the court with balls bouncing everywhere. Everyone filed through the line, and with each person's turn, his or her shoes squeaked and shuffled to get set for each crack at the ball.

POP! Thud. POP! Thud.

Squeak-squeak. POP! Thud.

"Short ball here!" Stacy yelled.

Squeak! POP! CLANK!

"Yeah! I got one!" Lifting his arms in the air with his mouth wide open, one boy looked back at the rest of the group, smiled, and shrugged his shoulders.

Stacy ordered, "That's ten push-ups! Go! One! Two! Three! Four!"

The boy laughed at first, but so did those starting their push-ups.

"We'll get you for this," a few said with a smile as they groaned.

This boy, whom I didn't know yet, smiled, but then he dropped his racquet. "C'mon. Let's do 'em together."

"Five… Six… Seven… Eight… Nine… Ten!" Stacy finished counting. "Awesome job, y'all! Now, stand back up! Here we go! Next person! Ball in!"

Stacy began feeding more tennis balls with her racquet to the other side of the net.

The sound of kernels popping was mixed with a bit of laughter this time.

Crack! POP! Whoosh! The ball whizzed right past a target. "Oh man! I almost had that one!" One girl stomped her foot, trying not to smile.

Squeak! POP! "Hey! I'm not a target, you guys!" Stacy leaned out of the way.

"We thought any standing object on your side was a target!" another boy joked.

"Ha! Good try, buddy. Here we go! Next ball! Next ball!"

POP! Squeak! POP! Whoosh! Thud.

"Check this out. Right target." One boy raised his eyebrows and stuck his tongue out the side of his lips. POP! CLANK! "Booya! Yessir!"

"Second ball!" Stacy shouted.

"Left target!" Squeak! POP! CLANK! "Booya!" He pumped his fist. "Jackpot!"

The group looked at Stacy with puppy-dog eyes and their hands in a prayer-like position. "No… please… no."

"Yes," Stacy pointed to the ground smiling, "that's twenty push-ups."

Laughing and moaning at the same time, everyone got down, including Mr. Sharpshooter.

"One! Two! Three!" All the way to twenty with many laughs from everyone along the way. "Alright! Y'all are awesome. Grab a sip of water and take a short break."

From my location a few courts away, I couldn't make out every word from their conversation, but it was obvious they all continued to smile and laugh. They kept motioning with shadow swings and acting out the recent double-target hit, pointing at where the boy had struck the baskets clean off their metal frames and shaking their heads in disbelief. More than one player approached him and gave him a high five.

Before they left the court, they all huddled into a circle and instead of everyone assembling their hands in the center, they each put in their racquets like a stack of pancakes. One person led the call. "Tennis on three! One! Two! Three!"

With all their might and in perfect unison as they raised their racquets to the sky, they called, "Tennis!"

Boy, they seemed to have a lot of fun together. I longed for that type of joy and excitement in my life and to share it with others.

Toward the end of summer, Stacy didn't want to keep me with all of the little kids, and I had become good enough to at least try and join in with the kids who had been playing tennis since they were five years old. So I began participating in their clinics.

I had become a good listener throughout the years as Gene did all the talking, so I was naturally an observer. What I began discovering very quickly was the same positive atmosphere I had initially noticed. There was constant smiling, laughing, and encouraging. Never did I ever hear people legitimately laughing at someone else.

"Guys, check out these new strings I got in my racquet." One girl pulled her racquet out of her bag. "They're hot pink! My favorite color! And nobody else has these yet. I'm so excited." They even matched her bright pink grip wrapped around the handle.

One boy interjected, "Actually," and he grabbed his racquet slowly out of his tennis backpack, "pink is the new black. Check these out!"

"What? No way!" She jumped for joy. "Twinsies!" She held her racquet over next to his, smiled, and gave the boy a fist bump.

I didn't quite understand why anyone needed new tennis strings, but I was more baffled nobody made fun of the boy for his pink strings. Gene would have eaten that up.

The new daily after-school clinic began, and there were so many players participating. The coaches spread everyone out amongst ten tennis courts with four players on each. The best players stayed on court one, the top court, and they went down the ladder dispersing the rest to their designated court. Nobody cared who was at the top or who was at the bottom. Everyone was there to work hard together.

The coaches announced the drills. "Okay. We need twenty shots in a row cross-court on both sides." The list went on for days. "You all have forty-five minutes to complete everything. Are there any comments or questions?"

"No sir," Campbell responded. He was the number one player. "Let's do this, guys." He encouraged everyone as we all headed out to our courts.

"Let's do it," others chimed in.

The coaches played some music to keep the vibe going.

"Sixteen!" POP! Thud. "Seventeen!" Whack! POP! Thud. Whack! Clank! "Ah!" Campbell missed a shot right before him and his partner reached twenty in a row.

"It's okay," his partner encouraged. "We can still do it. Here we go."

Campbell let out a deep breath as they began their trek to the top once again. "Eighteen!" POP! Thud. "Nineteen! Just make it! You got it!" Whack! POP! Thud. "Yes! Let's go!" Campbell ran up to the net and gave his partner a high five. "Thanks, man. Okay. Other side now."

Campbell was in high school, but the other boy was only in middle school like me.

Bullying seemed to be absent, and that was a shock. To learn there was a group of kids out there, who weren't even in the same grade level, and they were all being nice to one another? Apparently hanging out with each other outside of tennis too? It was surreal to me.

I had even begun to make new friends. One, in particular, was named Peyton. He stood out to me because even after having tennis clinic for hours in the hot sun, he went out of his way to practice with me for another thirty minutes to an hour after we were finished, like my dad had done with me.

POP. Thud. POP. Thud. As we rallied back and forth, Peyton said, "Man, Tyler, I've been playing since I was six years old. You are really good for having started only a couple months ago. And you're thirteen years old? Wow."

"Thanks, but it's because you're really helping show me the ins and outs of tennis. Plus, everyone seems to like you."

Peyton responded, "Oh, everyone here has fun together. It's a tight-knit community."

"Well, thank you for taking the time to stay and hit with me. I really appreciate it."

He didn't want to take any credit. "It's no problem for me. I love playing, and you're a cool guy. Dude. Check this out. Nobody's looking, are they?"

I peered around 360 degrees. "Nope. Don't think so. Why?"

"Do you think I can hit this ball across all four courts and over the fence?" He wiggled his eyebrows up and down a couple times and smiled. "It won't hurt anything. There's just a grassy field back there."

I shrugged my shoulders wondering if he should even do it, and before my shoulders came back down, Peyton tossed the ball into the air, let a scream out like a ninja, and POP! That ball went sailing through the air like an airplane zooming over the tops of the courts.

"Go… go… go! Yes! How about that? You wanna try?" Peyton's excitement was contagious, but I knew I wasn't going to partake.

I laughed. "No thank you, but that was cool."

"No worries, my good friend. Why don't you say we pack it up for the day?" Peyton didn't try and make me feel guilty.

"Sounds good," I said. But the best thing that sounded good was that last comment, 'my good friend.' I was becoming a part of a new world.

This wasn't a one-time thing. Peyton stayed with me after practice whenever I wanted. It helped me develop a very strong friendship with him. Life seemed to be good. During this one-on-one time with Peyton, I never heard him say anything negative about anybody else and that was so foreign to me, but I liked it. It was what I had always longed for but never felt I could find or achieve with a friend.

The kids who were the best tennis players, and seemed to be very popular, didn't act superior to the other tennis players who weren't as good. Peyton was someone who never beat the highest players and was lower with his tennis skills, but everyone loved him and he was friends with all of them. He wasn't made fun of for not being as talented as everyone else.

The most skilled of them all, Campbell, was not the type of leader I had ever experienced before in my life. Even though he and I were not very close, he didn't treat me like I was a nobody. Whenever we had practice, he spoke to me like I was a valid member of the group.

"What's up, Tyler? How was school today?" Campbell acknowledged me when I arrived on court.

"Good," I murmured but wanted to say the truth. I didn't have it in me to explain everything. Being spoken to with respect by a valid member of the tennis crew meant so much.

Later, when we came back together after completing our set of drills, Campbell addressed me again.

"Hey, Tyler. How did you guys do on your court? How far did you get on the list?"

I wanted to impress him, but I didn't want to lie. "Oh, we got halfway through." I shrugged my shoulders.

"That's actually pretty good." He gave me a high five.

This was so odd to me because I was coming from an environment where everyone had to watch their backs and prove themselves.

This newfound friend group was something I didn't ever want to leave. So I decided to make tennis my sport of choice for the next school year. I knew it would help me decompress from a day of being around negativity and finish on a positive note with positive people.

So that is exactly what I did. Every day after school, I was included as a member of the higher-level tennis clinic at the local Tennis Academy. My parents even followed my lead and decided to join as members even though they only ever took one tennis lesson. They were at least supporting my newfound passion. Things were looking up!

The only bad part... Gene was still in my life seventy-five percent of the day, and my eighth-grade year was looming around the corner.

CHAPTER 10

Two major events transpired before the end of middle school. The first one was positive, but the second, not so much.

At this point, the group of kids at the Tennis Academy did not consist of a single person from my school besides myself, and my guard slowly started to come down. At one moment that following year, Stacy created an opportunity for the tennis crew to go on a week-long trip to the west coast, and I really wanted to go. Not only would I miss an entire week of school away from the toxic social environment, but I wouldn't have to be around you-know-who.

My mom didn't really want me to miss school, and I have no idea why she let me go. I think I had to sign an agreement to complete all my schoolwork.

Anyway, this tennis trip ended up happening, and I had the best week of my life. I got to travel across the country while everyone was nice to each other the entire time. I was beginning to come out of my shell, and the other kids genuinely thought I was funny. That in itself was so odd to experience.

After the flight, we spent most of our time driving in a fifteen-passenger van. I was soaking it all in as we drove down the coastline. So many people were along the beach enjoying life. I spotted a family riding bikes, a man running with his water bottle in hand, a sporty girl roller blading, a group of friends playing volleyball, and much more. On the other side of this glass barrier in front of me was a busy world, and in this moment, it all appeared so bright and carefree. I was so mesmerized I was catching flies with my mouth.

"Tyler," Peyton snickered. "What are you looking at?"

My daydreaming was louder than his voice.

Peyton redirected my reverie. "Campbell, look at Tyler. He's so funny. Look what he's doing."

With my trap wide open, I halfway snapped out of it and raised my eyebrows as I turned toward Peyton and Campbell. I didn't catch myself almost drooling. *Did he just say I was funny?*

Campbell and everyone erupted. "Oh my gosh! Tyler!"

Peyton couldn't contain himself. "Tyler! Can you do that again? You are hilarious!"

"Do what?" I was confused. Not only did I not know what I had done, but my lens was unclear because they genuinely wanted more. They weren't laughing at me. Peyton and the crew honestly believed when I lost my focus and stared out the window with my mouth wide open looking back at them with the same expression, it was a natural comedy act.

"That look you gave us!" Campbell roared, slapping his thigh.

I rolled with it. "Okay. Check this." Gazing back out the window and opening the fly trap once more, I said, "Call my name."

They were already falling over. "We can't!"

Peyton attempted through his cackles, "T-T-Tyler."

In one fell swoop, I rotated my head toward them, but this time, I buttered up the blank stare just a bit, and they ate it right up. The van shook like an earthquake from all the hoots and hollers echoing and bouncing off the walls and made its way into my heart, reviving my soul.

Once I discovered I mattered to this group of people, I knew I wanted more, and there was no way I was letting go.

Typically, around what's-his-name's crowd back home, I tended to laugh at a lot of stuff, but if I laughed at someone's joke, the immediate response was something like, "That's not funny." They tried to make me feel bad for simply responding to somebody's joke in a positive manner. So when they did that, I didn't even think twice about actually trying to make someone laugh myself because I was deemed as definitely not funny either.

During our tennis excursion, I didn't hold back. I didn't realize this until later, but I felt truly uninhibited.

"Guys, look at this. I'm starting a new trend." Peyton had his shirt and shorts on backward and the goofiest look on his face.

I squawked loudly. "That's awesome!"

To my utter bewilderment, everyone lost it again but not because of Peyton's antics.

The entire group was having side stitches.

"Tyler! Oh my gosh! Your laugh!" Peyton shouted. "Do it again!"

I wasn't sure how to repeat this action because the first time was authentic. I couldn't fake my normal laugh. I simply shrugged my shoulders and smiled.

What in the world is happening? They're enjoying my stares. They're encouraging my laugh. They're accepting me.

One afternoon, when we were playing some matches against the locals from that area, everyone else was finished, but I hadn't quite sealed the deal yet. Peyton, Campbell, and the others came over to support me.

A shot of nerves hit me because I was still fairly new to the game. My skill wasn't at the same level as my opponent. He cranked a huge forehand, and I caught it late, accidentally hitting it over the side fence.

"Sorry. It's okay. I still have one here." I held up the ball in my left hand preparing to serve the next point.

"I got it!" Peyton shouted. "Incoming!" He sailed it back over the fence toward me. With little time to react, I looked up and saw the ball falling quickly toward my left side. I didn't have time to reach over with my racquet, and I already had one tennis ball in my left hand. In a split second, I chose to toss the ball from my hand a few feet into the air so I could catch the other one. After I caught it, I proceeded to juggle the two tennis balls in my left hand until I felt like I had gained control back. Then I let one of them hit the ground and started to softly bounce it with my racquet while I housed the other one in my left pocket.

CLAP... CLAP...

It started slow, but then I looked up realizing the entire sideline was full of players from both groups, and they all started cheering like I had won an amazing point.

"Yay, Tyler!" Campbell shouted and clapped.

"Wow. Did you know he could do that?" A player not from our group leaned over to Peyton to ask him.

"Of course I did!" Peyton lied and kindly popped his palm on this guy's back. "That's Tyler. He is amazing."

I lost the next few points and the match. After shaking hands, I slouched over to the sideline.

"Yo! Tyler! That was great!" Campbell was smiling from ear to ear.

I was wondering what he was talking about because I had just lost, not to mention in front of everyone.

"You didn't tell us you could juggle," Peyton whispered and peered over his shoulder to make sure that one boy couldn't hear him, "let alone with your opposite hand. I can barely play tennis with my dominant hand."

These types of comments were the ones I had been missing my whole life. I was ready to add these to the pool of words swimming around in my head. There was a strong hope these new ones would cause the negative ones from my past to sink and disappear into the depths forever.

All in all, the trip was a complete game changer for me. I was essentially a part of the tennis crew now, and I didn't even really have to try. All I had to do was go on the trip. These were my new real friends.

When I was about to become a high schooler, one of the cool things to do was go to the local high school football games. This consisted of going to the game and walking laps with "friends," while never actually watching a second of football. It was purely social time, nothing else.

Another thing that happened in middle and high school was boys often messed with one another in a "joking" manner, a little bit more than they had in the past. Um... remember the scissors? I was sure that was just supposed to be a joke, right? However, not everyone took them as something funny.

One of the pranks at the time was to "pants" each other. However, I felt like if I did that to someone, I would get beat up. It seemed to only be okay for the most popular kids to prey on the weak because they couldn't retaliate.

It was Friday night, and the sun hadn't yet set over the horizon. You could hear the announcer on the loudspeaker calling the game and the whistles of the referees on the playing field. Helmets hitting one another. Cheers in the crowd. The smell of fresh popcorn filled the early evening air. And then there was our little middle-school group, walking laps around the outside of the track.

It was all the boys and all the girls, not to mention Susan, now the hottest girl in our class, whom all the boys liked at this point. Her olive skin glowed in the sunset. She didn't have to dress nice to look good with her pulled-back ponytail, t-shirt, shorts, and one too many bracelets wrapped around her wrist.

"Guys, let's go this way." Gene directed the pack while I was near the caboose.

Kevin lifted his nose and started sniffing like a hunting dog. "You smell that?" He closed his eyes and smirked on one side of his mouth. "I'm following that scent right to the concession stand. I'm starving."

"Oink!" someone snorted. A few soft snickers followed.

"Huh?" Kevin tilted his head.

Crews reached over and poked Kevin in the stomach and laughed.

Kevin shoved Crews backward just a hair. "Very funny." Then he reached out and poked Crews in the belly too.

They proceeded to joust each other like medieval warriors until Crews attempted to lift up Kevin's shirt for one more quick jab, but Kevin cried out, "Okay! Truce!" He couldn't fathom the girls seeing his stomach.

"That's right! Truce," Crews agreed just in time.

He was lucky Kevin didn't body slam him into the ground like a professional wrestler. Maybe my punch hadn't weighed heavy enough on Crews's mind to make him leave people alone.

Jackson nudged both of them apart and jostled his way toward the front and threw his arm around Gene's shoulder as everyone continued walking. He leaned in, cupped his hands next to Gene's ear for a few seconds, and whispered something. They both tilted their heads back and howled like a couple of hyenas.

I figured they had to be making fun of Kevin. What else would they be doing?

In one big mass, we walked and talked without ever really stopping. In the midst of one of our laps, everyone had come to a halt near the bleachers to discuss something. I was too busy lost in a daydream about Susan, wondering what could have been if she had ever said "Yes" all those years ago.

I faded away into my own thoughts. "Tyler, I like your shirt. It's cute. Do you want to walk with me?" Susan's imaginary voice was making my dreams come true.

Oh my. No way. I mean, yes. Yes way! Yes! Yes, I will walk with you, Susan!

"Will you hold my hand?" She smiled, leaned her cheek into her own shoulder, and batted her eyelashes.

I held out my hand with my fingers splayed open so she could rest her hand in mine.

CRASH!!

FWEET!!!

One player's helmet flew off, and the referee's whistle blasted my eardrums. He launched a penalty flag into the air. I flinched hard and blinked, coming back into reality and registering Susan was nowhere near me, or at least not close enough to be holding my hand. Maybe one day.

In middle school, boys and girls typically remained separate. So even though we walked as a group, the girls were together in one area, and the boys were in another.

Since we had parked right next to the stands, some of the boys had stopped behind me to check out what was taking place on the field.

Jackson yelled, "Take him out! That's targeting!"

"Do you think they'll eject him?" Kevin asked.

"They better," Gene snarled. "I hate players like that."

Jackson leaned closely into Gene again to tell him something. I wasn't very concerned, so I took this extra time to see if my love was waiting for me.

I stood there just feeling like everything was going so well and everyone was having a good time. Susan was standing across from me, but this time, in real life, she was looking directly at me and smiling. Then, as I slowly vanished back into daydreaming about her being my girlfriend like everyone else did...

WOOSH!

My shorts were on the ground around my ankles. Ah! I pulled those puppies back up as fast as I could. My face immediately turned red and my heart began to beat a mile a minute in my chest.

You would've thought another punch to the perpetrator was coming, but I knew I couldn't do anything like that again, especially at a major football event like this with so many people witnessing my actions. At the time, believe it or not, I wasn't angry. Yes, I was completely caught off guard, and yes, I was embarrassed because my "girlfriend" along with all the rest of the girls in class were all right there!

My boxers had remained intact. Thank God. However, the most embarrassing thing for me as a new tennis player was my major farmer's tan. My calves were caramel gold, yet my thighs were as white as the moon.

In that moment, I didn't retreat. I tried to "be one of the boys" and laugh it off. I knew I couldn't return the favor to the boy who had done it because he was one of the strongest boys in the grade, and he would have definitely hurt me.

So you know what I did? I tied my shorts as tight as I could as we continued our walk, and in addition to that, I never let go of the waistband with one of my hands for the rest of the night. My grip was so tight on my own shorts that if anyone had tried to pants me again, the only way my shorts would hit the ground would be because they ripped in half.

I know that all sounds hilarious, and that I took it all in stride, but if we got back to the emotional side of things, I was losing, again. For me to walk around like that the remaining two hours of the game... now that was sad. Who does that? Most boys would just "play" back, but I wasn't like that. I didn't like that. I never considered treating somebody else in that manner.

This event might have been comical to read about, but it was one of the major defining moments of my eighth-grade year. So much so that it would play into where I would ultimately decide to go to high school.

CHAPTER 11

Every year of my educational life, we took standardized tests in school. Whenever the scores came in and I looked at the chart and tried to comprehend it, I noticed spelling was in a completely different column than reading, math, and everything else. Why? Because apparently, based on my results, all I knew how to do was spell. If it was possible to fail a standardized test, I did it every year. According to my scores, I was incapable of doing very much else. Unfortunately, I was unsure about how to capitalize on the talent I did have.

Ms. Baker, our English teacher, lined the entire class around the room for the annual spelling bee. If you got it correct, you went to the end of the line, and the next person stepped up to the hot seat. Those who misspelled a word had to take the walk of shame right to their desk. This process occurred until there was one student left standing. Whoever won got to represent the class in front of the entire school.

"Gene," Ms. Baker called. "Your word is 'disgusting.' Please spell disgusting."

He began sounding it out to himself. "Dis-kus-ting." Trying to buy himself some time, he wrote the letters in the air with his fingers.

Jackson nudged Gene and whispered, "Ask for a definition."

Gene turned over his shoulder and mumbled back, "Shut up. I got this, dude."

Unable to clearly hear their dialogue, Ms. Baker asked, "Gene, are you ready?"

Jackson murmured low enough Ms. Baker couldn't discern his words. "Are you disgusting?" He was referring to her.

Gene snickered and replied, "Yes. Dis-kus-ting. D-i-s-k-u-s-t-i-n-g. Disgusting."

Then we waited in silence for three seconds.

DING! Ms. Baker hit the bell on her desk and its sound reverberated around the room. In conjunction with the protocols at the national spelling bee, this meant Gene had spelled the word incorrectly. It must have been the nice way of saying, "You're wrong."

"Great try, Gene. You were so close. You may have a seat." Ms. Baker continued down the line. "Jackson, please spell 'aptitude.'"

"Wow. That's so easy. Attitude." And before Ms. Baker could intervene, Jackson confidently spelled the word he thought she said. "A-t-t-i-t-u-d-e. Bam! That's what's up!" He turned around to the person behind him and threw his chin up with a strong belief in himself. "Man, if it's going to be that ea—"

DING!

Jackson's head spun on a swivel as he raised one eyebrow. "What? That's how you spell attitude. I know how to spell attitude, Ms. Baker. Don't make me look it up and prove you wrong."

Very calmly, Ms. Baker responded, "I'm very sorry, Jackson, but the word was aptitude, not attitude. You spoke too soon before I could repeat the word more clearly. According to the rules, you are out. Please have a—"

"Oh my gahhh!" Jackson threw his hands in the air. "This is ridiculous. I swear . . ." He huffed but stopped himself before he got into trouble.

He marched away and plopped down next to Gene in the back of the class, near the end of the line where I was waiting for my turn.

"This whole thing is so dumb," Gene muttered to Jackson. "Only nerds were born for competitions like this. What difference does one stupid letter make?"

Neither of you would be saying that if you had spelled your words correctly.

Hearing their comments made me second-guess my efforts for a moment. I wanted to do well because I knew I could.

As the spelling bee proceeded, some students heard the DING of death while others pranced to the end of the line in a celebratory fashion. Finally, it was my turn.

Ms. Baker addressed me. "Tyler, your word is 'deceitful.' I'll say that one more time, 'deceitful.'"

Okay. I actually know this. It has a 'c' with an 's' sound, and in this case, the 'e' goes before the 'i' like in 'receive.'

I hesitated for a moment but then remembered I wanted to show what I could do.

"Yes, ma'am," I answered. I looked Ms. Baker right in the eyes. "De-seet-full. D-e-c-e-i-t-f-u-l. Deceitful." I nodded and waited.

One... Two... Three . . .

"That is correct. Amazing job, Tyler. That was a tough first word. Bravo. You can go to the end of the line."

As I turned around and made the trek, I kept my head down trying to block out Gene and Jackson.

"I cannot believe this. She is so dumb. All she does is give the easy words to everyone else." Gene shook his head and rolled his eyes.

Jackson agreed. "Yeah. Look who's up now."

It was Lauren, the smartest student in the grade in every class. She always got the highest score on everything.

"She thinks she is so much better than everyone else," Gene commented. "She's so irritating."

"If there's one thing, it's that she's uglier than everyone else," Jackson whispered and chortled softly. He elbowed Gene gently, "Am I right?"

Gene laughed. "Exactly. This contest was made for ugly and annoying people. Who would even waste their time?"

Of course, Lauren spelled her word correctly and trotted to the end.

With about seven students remaining, I was back at the front again.

"Tyler, your new word is 'suspicious,'" Ms. Baker called out loud and clear.

I knew this one too. It was easy for me, but two other words were ringing in my ears: ugly and annoying.

There was only one thing to do.

"Yes, Ms. Baker. Suh-spi-shuss." I acted as if I was trying to write it on the palm of my hand when really, I knew what I was going to do.

In my head, I was aware this word ended with -i-o-u-s, but I only saw one way to remove myself from this word and from this line of contestants, and that was to omit the letter "i" toward the end because I no longer had the desire to be the last one standing. Not only did I not want to be considered any of those things Gene and Jackson had mentioned, but I also knew I couldn't survive the stage fright if I won and had to participate in front of the entire school.

I cleared my throat and swallowed. "Suh-spi-shuss. S-u-s-p-i-c-o-u-s. Suspicious." I knew exactly what I had done and patiently waited for the bell, but I raised my eyebrows to put on like maybe I was right when I knew I wasn't.

DING!

"That's alright, Tyler. Good try. It's -i-o-u-s, dear," Ms. Baker said.

I shrugged my shoulders, played it off like it was no big deal, and took a seat to watch the remainder of the event until, ultimately, Lauren won.

When she represented our class at the grand finale in the gym, she was eliminated on her second word, which I knew how to spell but never told anyone.

Even though I wasn't the strongest student in everything like Lauren, I still made good grades. If I slacked off a little, I got As, Bs, and one C per quarter. I think I only achieved straight As once in my life in middle school. The only problem was this: to get into a private high school, I had to take a standardized test in order to proceed along that journey.

There were only two options for high school: the all-boys school where we went to watch the football games, and the co-ed school. My decision was made very quickly. I wanted to go to the co-ed school. Duh.

Why? Because Gene was for sure going to the all-boys school. It was the more popular school with a successful competitive sports background. The co-ed school was the unpopular school that never won in sports and was made fun of by others. You would have thought it was the other way around, but it was not.

This was my golden ticket to separate myself completely from Gene and start a new life. Patience and hope kicked in because I still had to take the big test first, get accepted into the school, and then I could decide.

The entrance exam took place within each of the high schools. The classroom air conditioners were set to sixty-eight degrees or lower. All the posters on the walls were covered with large sheets of paper and duct tape on the corners. Nothing was to remain visible as something that could possibly assist with answering a test question. Nobody was even talking to one another before we started because the stakes were high. The first test was at the all-boys school. At least this would be the only time I'd ever be here for anything.

"I am now passing out a scratch sheet of paper and a number two pencil. Do not break the seal along the edge of your test booklet until I tell you to do so." The testing proctor was cold and serious. Her high heels made a clatter on the hard, tile flooring as she made her way around the room.

In a relaxed manner, I patiently waited until the pencil rattled the top of my metal desk. It was like she was trying to make us nervous, but I wasn't fazed. My mind had other plans.

"Hey! What do you think you're doing?" She scowled at one boy who had accidentally torn the seal on his test.

He stared at her like a deer in headlights. "Umm. I didn't know." He put his hands in the air to try and protect his innocence.

"Didn't know?" she said. "What part of 'don't break the seal' do y'all not understand?"

Y'all? This lady wasn't going to get into my head though because this test was for the all-boys school, and I couldn't have cared less how well I did, but I was still going to try. A part of me always wanted to improve my poor test-taking history. I didn't particularly enjoy having that stamp on my back.

"Gentlemen, you may now break the seal and open to the first page while I read the instructions. All answers must be recorded in the answer document. Please make sure your name and information are correct. Raise your hand if it is not. This assessment will measure your proficiency in various subject areas, and your level of achievement will determine your status of entry into this school. You will have exactly two hours to complete all sections. I will tell you when there are five minutes remaining. If you finish early, you may go back and check your work. Are there any questions?" She waited a few seconds, raised her eyebrows, and nodded. "Please turn the page, and you may begin."

My left thumb dug under the bottom right corner of the page. I slowly flipped it to the left and the air escaped from below as it gently fell on top of the one beneath it. I wished I could flee from this room in a similar brisk manner before the pressure of life could come raining down on top of me.

Ticktock. Ticktock. The clock on the wall clicked continuously with only some slight shuffling in a chair every now and then. All heads remained looking down but also moved left and right like a tennis match when they changed from viewing the test booklet to bubbling in a response on the answer document.

After what felt like a half hour, the lady announced, "Gentlemen, you have five minutes remaining." And shortly thereafter, "Put your pencils down. Close your test booklets. You have now completed the entrance exam. You will receive notification in the mail about your results. Thank you for coming."

I let out a sigh of relief, and the legs of the chair screeched on the floor as I scooched backward to stand. I hoped these were going to be my final footsteps inside this building. I walked right out of there and didn't look back.

One week later, it was time to give it everything I had to pass the exam to be accepted into the co-ed school where I knew my life was going to change.

The testing room wasn't as chilly this time, but I was also sweating under my shirt a little, praying for my brain to deliver the right answers into the palm of my hand. I was so focused this time. I never heard a sound until the proctor instructed us, "Stop. Everyone, pencils down. That is the end of the test."

I wiped my brow, sunk a little lower in my chair, and blew outward as my lips fluttered against one another.

The proctor said, "Please be patient until we can complete the process of family interviews on our special evening coming up in a couple weeks. We hope to see all of you soon."

When I was leaving the classroom and walking down the hallway, I imagined my new life. It was going to be amazing. Shortly after, my mom picked me up, and in the car on the way home, I closed my eyes to picture it once again. Everyone was smiling and enjoying each other's company. There were no butterflies in my stomach because Gene was nowhere to be seen or heard. He was at the other school. Far, far away.

Then, after a couple weeks ticked off the calendar, I was back.

The principal welcomed the families, "Good evening, everyone! We are so excited for all of you to be here with us tonight. We cannot express how grateful we are to consider having you and your child join our wonderful school. In just a moment, each family will have their own private interview conducted by one of our very own teachers. If you take a look at your personal invitation, you will see a room number on there with a map of the school on the back. Please find your room, and also, don't forget to have fun."

Fun? Are you serious? This is a matter of a new life and a slow death.

My parents and I made our way to our assigned classroom.

"Hello!" A very welcoming, young, and full-of-life teacher ushered us to a few seats. She was smiling from ear to ear. "Tyler, right? How are you doing? I am so excited to meet you!" She had a genuine care in her voice, but she also had an odd aura surrounding her. The over-exuberant cheerfulness was masking something, but I had no idea what.

This was also an interview of her first impression of us, so I responded, "Hi. It's nice to meet you too. Thank you for having us. We truly appreciate how welcoming everyone is here."

"Oh, yes. That is probably my favorite trait about this school, the warm and inviting environment. It's contagious!" She grinned.

"It sounds really nice. So I think they said you are going to take us on a tour?" I was curious.

"Well," she stumbled. "Umm… there's one thing we have to do first." She went behind her desk and pulled out the file drawer. Like a lobster, she clawed one file and laid it down on the desk in front of all of us."

"What is this?" I asked.

"The documents inside this folder contain your entrance exam information as well as the school's simulated schedule for you next year." She had locked in on her poker face for some reason.

I sat up straight. "Oh! So we need to see what the schedule says before we take our tour. I understand."

She began digging out the pieces of paper one by one and spreading them out onto the larger table where we were sitting.

"These are Tyler's test results," she said.

It was a bit confusing with a bunch of numbers and bar graphs everywhere. I didn't really care what it all meant. I was ready to go on the tour to see my future.

"Based on Tyler's data, here is his schedule for summer school." She braced for the reaction.

"What? Summer school? Wait a minute. Why? I don't get it," I said.

"According to this information," she explained, "Tyler's performance on the entrance exam indicates he will need to attend summer school to prove he is capable of handling the academic load at our school."

My mom jumped in with a question I never thought of asking. "And how long is summer school?"

"Our program runs five days a week, all day long, for the months of June and July."

My heart fell out of my chest, and then this lady stepped on it as she continued.

"Also, this other paper, which is his incomplete mock schedule for next school year, specifies that even if Tyler performs well in summer school, he will begin next fall semester in remedial classes. This means it will take longer for him to graduate because these classes are not worth any credit toward graduation."

So I would be going to school for a while for no reason? This is ridiculous.

My parents nodded because they understood it was protocol, but I didn't need this getting in the way of setting me free.

"We wanted to make you aware of this today so you could better comprehend the reason for having a strong foundation before making your official decision to join our school."

But wait. I already decided. I thought I was going to this school.

My heart was now in pieces. I couldn't speak anymore.

My dad stepped in. "I think we will need some time to process this as a family. We will take all of this into consideration before making our final selection on a school. Thank you so much for having us this evening."

I blinked, and we were gone. The only thing I had to look forward to was a week off of school for spring break and some time to get away.

The following week, my dad and I drove seven hours on the open road to my grandparents' house. I had a lot of time to think.

Every now and then, Dad broke the silence. "Tyler, no matter what decision we make about school, I know you tried your best on the test. As long as you keep putting your best foot forward, that's all I could ever ask. Don't be down on yourself, okay? Your mom and I simply want what's best for you."

"Thanks." I stared out the window.

Unbeknownst to him, I wasn't concerned about my score anymore, but rather, the lingering possible effect. I kept trying to convince myself that two full months of summer school for five days a week from morning to afternoon followed by remedial classes wasn't as bad as it sounded. But it was. It wasn't only bad. It was awful, dreadful, abominable!

As an eighth-grade adolescent, I didn't want to do the above-mentioned list immediately after graduating from middle school no matter how badly I wanted to steer as far away from Gene as possible.

While Dad and I were visiting my grandparents, my mom called us a little after dinnertime one evening.

"Mhm. Okay. Yeah." My dad was giving his usual phone conversation responses to my mom until it was my turn. "Got it. Okay. Here's Tyler." He passed me the phone.

"Hey, Mom."

"How's my baby boy? I've missed you! Are you having so much fun?" She was extra bubbly, but Mom wasn't like that.

"I'm fine. It's been nice to get away for a bit, but not from you, of course!" I saved myself.

"Aren't you sweet?" I felt her smiling. "Guess what? A special letter came in the mail today." She added a little extra emphasis on *letter*. This seemed like good news she was waiting to share with me.

"Oh, really? What kind of special letter?" I wondered. I wasn't really expecting anything in the mail.

"Well, this is a letter pertaining to your entrance exam for the all-boys school." Again, the inflection in her voice had a positive vibe.

I listened intently as she continued, "It states that after careful consideration, you have earned yourself a spot on the waiting list."

Even though I didn't want to go to this school, I hoped my testing history would change for the better.

My mom attempted to make me feel better. "Here's some good news. It says if you get accepted, you will have to attend summer school—"

"What? How is that good news?"

"If you would let me finish, you would find out." She somehow gave me that motherly look through the phone. "It states if you receive notification to attend summer school, their schedule is five days a week for only half a day each time, and it only lasts the month of June. Then, if you perform well, you will be accepted into the school."

O… M… G… are you serious? How could this be happening to me? I was supposed to be leaving Gene. What did I do to deserve this? I didn't want to go to the all-boys school for one reason, but with this summer school lineup ahead of me, it seemed like the all-boys school was the way to go.

I don't remember finishing that phone conversation, and the rest of my trip was a blur. I couldn't stop thinking about this terrible situation. Once I arrived back home, I saw the letter on the counter in the kitchen. I stared at it for a very long time as I weighed which of my options was worse: giving away my entire summer immediately after eighth-grade graduation plus credit-less remedial classes, or losing only a third of my summer and having to deal with Gene for what felt like just a little bit longer. I had already survived nine years, but every time I imagined how it might be, my stomach churned.

My mom had always wanted me to go to the all-boys school. It was the stronger academic school, and she had the means to pay for me to receive a great education, so that's what she wanted. However, she knew I didn't want to go there. I wasn't quite sure if she knew why, but I knew, and it made me so uneasy thinking I would continue for the next four years, potentially walking the same halls and sitting in the same classes as Gene once again.

After complaining to my mom for a quick minute about not wanting to go there, she gave me a third option. She said I could go to the local public high school I was zoned for if I really didn't want to go to this school.

My mind started playing unfounded visuals of possible fist-fights and bullying 24/7. I had grown up in the private-school bubble, and I had only seen somebody get punched maybe twice in my entire life, and I was one of those throwing the punch. I had never witnessed a true fight. I felt like if I went to public school, I wouldn't survive. It seemed like I would be even more on guard than I already was. If the bullying I was witnessing in private school took this much of a toll on me, then what would the public-school world do to me? My heart wanted to choose public school, but my mind never allowed me. There was no way it was actually going to happen. It was too far out of my comfort zone.

I gave in and told my mom I'd go to the all-boys summer school. She was very happy, I think.

As I walked into the upstairs classroom on the first day of summer school, my eyes quickly scanned the room of about twenty boys who were there for the math class.

No... way . . .

Gene was in the class! He got put on the waiting list too! That meant he was as dumb as me! He wouldn't be able to make fun of me for having to do summer school because he had to take it too! Ha!

I ended up sitting next to him because what do you do when you don't know anybody else in the room? You sit with the people you know.

As summer school ran its course, I knew I had to perform because if I did not get into this school, I was going to the public high school, and that scared me more than being around Gene. Therefore, I passed with flying colors. There was only math, reading, and study skills. I got an A in all of them. It was a piece of cake, honestly. Unfortunately, this meant that similar to how I was in every summer school class with Gene, the same would probably ensue as we began school in the fall.

Shrug.

At least I still had tennis to keep me grounded. It was all I had to keep a positive mindset on life.

CHAPTER 12

I was stuck. There was no going back now. Freshman year kicked off, and I probably had over half of my classes alongside my lifelong bully. He was in rare form in high school, and the comments and conversations became more hurtful with age. It really began to bother me to the point where I felt trapped.

In case you forgot, the way in which I felt like I survived was by letting Gene feel like I always agreed with his opinion or by laughing at what he laughed at for the most part. By no means was it even close to the same level as him, but it was more just giving him the reassurance he desired about the things he said. So if he made a comment about somebody else and laughed and then turned to me, I most likely gave a half smile and a very small "ha" with my mouth closed, all while feeling guilty for even doing so.

Since we were now in high school, there were all these new people we had never been around before, and Gene had new victims upon which to prey. I continuously had that guilty feeling grabbing my stomach every time I reaffirmed Gene's comments.

"He's so stupid."

"I can't believe he wore that."

"I hate him."

"I hate that."

"That is so gay."

"That movie sucked."

"I hate that show. Let's watch . . ."

"She's ugly."

"He thinks he's so cool."

I could go on forever. We'll stop right there because I'd have to write a separate book for all the comments.

It was one day in freshman algebra class, which was my specialty. We sat in individual desks that were in rows facing the front of the room. I sat one row behind Gene and to the right. I was about four rows deep. There was no way a teacher would be able to hear the things Gene could say about her, or about anyone.

Then, one day, I did something I had never done before . . .

My inability to prevent myself from reacting to Gene's words by always giving him reassurance was getting to me. The angel on my shoulder was wagging her finger in my face and shaking her head in disappointment. I looked back at her, nodded, and lowered my chin. Something had to be done.

I imagined I was a thoroughbred about to be released from the starting blocks of the biggest race of my life, but the only way to win was to keep my blinders on and look straight ahead. This wasn't about speed, but rather, self-discipline and focus. Gene was bound to make a mistake before crossing the finish line.

My desk was my starting stall. My nerves shimmied and jostled about in my stomach waiting for the bell for class to start.

BRRRING!

The teacher began class. "Good afternoon, gentlemen. Who remembers what we did yesterday?"

A single hand shot in the air.

Gene tried to whisper, "I know what he did yesterday," and pointed to the boy in front of me who didn't realize he was being targeted. This particular boy was a bit heavier than most of the other boys, and I already felt bad for him just by looking at him. I knew bullies picked on the weak, but this wasn't fair. To make fun of him was downright awful.

I blinked hard and zoomed in on the teacher. *Don't do it. Run straight. Keep your eyes on the prize. Please don't look at me.*

"Only one hand? Gentleman, none of you except Peter can recall what we did yesterday?"

Gene couldn't help himself, and in another faint voice said, "This guy had one too many chips yesterday." Gene pointed with his head this time.

Oh my gosh. Are you serious right now? Why?

The boy still had no idea.

Please don't. Just don't turn around. As long as he doesn't look at me, I can do this.

Without moving a muscle, I tried to steer my eyes toward Peter, who was one row to my right.

"Ooo! Ooo! Me! I know! Please pick me," Peter begged.

"Okay, Peter. Go ahead." The teacher gave in.

"Yesterday we talked about volume."

"That is correct, Peter. Thank you for remembering. Do you happen to know what we said the definition of volume was?" She probed for more information.

Peter jumped right in. "Of course. Volume is a three-dimensional space that is taken up by an object. You're welcome." He smiled.

"Like this guy." Gene pointed again. "He's taking up a lot of space."

I tightened my blinders because I knew it was coming. As Gene continued to laugh, he turned his head over his right shoulder to snicker and get that reassuring chuckle from me.

A rush of nerves scattered throughout my body like pins and needles because I knew what I needed to do, and that was not to react.

My heart started beating even harder, and I could feel my body turning warm.

I didn't laugh.

I didn't even look his direction.

Out of my peripheral vision, I could see Gene still glancing in my direction and chuckling, but he began to notice I wasn't reacting. I remained tunnel-vision focused on the front of the room even though he continued to check if I was going to acknowledge him. I had already made my choice, and there was no turning back.

The little angel on my shoulder was my jockey, and she urged me down the homestretch to help me successfully cross the finish line.

Despite the self-proclaimed victory, my stomach was still uneasy.

While the teacher taught for the remainder of class, Gene didn't say a word with a straight look on his face. He took notes and paid attention, but it was very unsettling not knowing what was going on in his mind after I had refused to bow to the king himself.

BRRRING!

"Boys, don't forget your homework tonight! We have a quiz in a couple of days!" The teacher talked over the squeaking of chair legs on the floors.

Gene shot out of his chair and bolted out of the room for the next class, but I took my time as I continued to play the scene over and over in my head.

Did I really just do that?

This was a major turning point in my life around Gene. It was the first time I had made a decision not to fulfill his ego while in his presence, and the decision was not based on what he would think. It was the first time I wasn't a follower, and I did not give him that same reassurance I always had in the past.

Only time would tell if anything would come of this rebellious moment.

As I continued forward, I refrained from reaffirming Gene's comments. I didn't laugh at things he said, and I didn't even look his direction. That was even the case as I still sat next to him in some of the other classes.

One day in social studies class, we had a substitute teacher. However, the sub was not an outsider. It was another teacher from within the building who taught the older grade levels. In general, when there was a substitute, we didn't really have class.

I remember the teacher's desk was in the front left corner of the room. Gene was sitting about five feet away from this area with Kevin in the next seat to his right. I reluctantly sat in the very next spot. The student seating area was split down the middle by a ten-foot gap where our usual teacher marched back and forth while lecturing. Two rows of student desks faced each other from opposite sides of the room.

The substitute gave instructions. "Gentlemen, your teacher had to leave early today for a doctor's appointment. It was sort of last minute. He says you know what you need to be working on, so I expect you to complete whatever it is that he wants you to accomplish and to not get too loud."

The sub simply sat back down at the teacher's desk and worked on something for the duration of that class period while everyone else was supposed to be doing their work.

Very quickly after the sub adjusted his glasses and dug his nose into his pile of papers to grade, many boys decided to do anything but complete their work. However, everyone was meeting his request of not turning the volume up too high, so he wasn't bothered by the defiant work environment.

While others whispered around the room, Gene and Kevin began a discussion about a boy named Nolan who had previously gone to our old school and was a major target for bullying.

Gene started. "Do you remember Nolan?"

"Oh yeah." Kevin chuckled.

"He was so weird," Gene said. "What about the time he cried because nobody picked him for their team at recess?"

Kevin laughed. "Wow. I know."

"What a total wuss. It was just recess." Gene shook his head.

"I know. Seriously," Kevin said.

"Do you remember how he smelled?" Gene pinched his nose. "Oh my gosh. I'm going to throw up just thinking about it. No wonder nobody showed up to his birthday party that one year."

"Yeah. He was an odd one for sure," Kevin concurred.

As I sat in my chair transcribing their conversation into my mind, I was at a loss because Kevin was also a target for bullying due to his weight. However, Kevin knew he had to join Gene instead of fight against him. So the short discussion that consisted of making fun of Nolan turned into a very long exchange. They were reminiscing about things that had happened in the past and laughed about it the entire class period.

As the conversation grew, I faked like I was doing my work, but instead, my ears were wide open the whole time—how could they not be? Gene and Kevin were making fun of somebody, and they weren't even trying to hide it. I also sat there wondering how I was still the only person in this world who was aware of the hurt Gene and his followers spread every single day? Conversations like this were happening all the time. I couldn't believe the substitute teacher didn't hear anything they were saying. My insides were fuming.

BRRRING!

The bell rang, and everyone got up from their desks. Voices started getting louder as the rush of students headed toward the doorway, but Gene and Kevin were casually gathering their things because they were still snickering about Nolan.

The teacher cleared his throat. "Excuse me, boys," he said in a fairly serious tone.

It seemed he was glaring at all three of us, but I knew I wasn't a part of this team anymore.

Oh my gosh. Did he hear them?

He addressed Gene and Kevin. "Do you realize you just spent an entire hour of your life making fun of another person?" He shook his head.

Yes! OMG! Finally! Someone else knows!

Without giving any official punishment, the teacher walked out to go back to his assigned classroom.

As soon as he exited, Gene mocked the teacher. "Oh my! I'm so scared!" He put his hands on the side of his cheeks with his mouth wide open.

Kevin added, "What an idiot."

"Yeah. He needs to mind his own business."

They both tilted their heads back and laughed as they entered the busy hallway to continue with the rest of their day.

Like I said before, Gene knew how to beat the system and never feel bad about anything. The general population believed bullying was only when someone was specifically being targeted by an intimidator who directly picked on other people through physical or mental abuse. Gene did not fit this description, yet I strongly believed he had grown into one of the most dangerous types of bullies to ever exist. He did all of his work behind-the-scenes without ever laying a hand on anyone.

He was like a computer hacker who knew how to convince others to give him all their money through a transaction they never intended on making, and before they knew it, they had either become a hacker themselves or they were so deep in a hole it was impossible to climb out. For me, it was like I was still losing my money when I didn't have any left to give. Maybe I was buried a lot further than other victims because, many times, I was sitting in the room witnessing Gene cause so much pain toward others without their being physically present. And because they weren't in immediate earshot of all the comments, Gene never showed remorse. The worst part was fear preventing me from telling him to stop.

Since we were only about one month into school when the events in algebra and social studies happened, I decided the best way for me to fight back was to not be anything like Gene, and in order for me to do that, I was never going to do anything Gene did, especially when it involved laughing at the expense of others. This also meant if Gene went to a school football game or joined a sporting team, I was not going to do that. As freshman year proceeded, I did not attend any social events that were put on by the school because Gene would be present. If there was a party at someone's house, like a true high school party, I was not there because I knew he would be. I didn't want to emulate his lifestyle or support his behavior.

Even though I had made this decision, which did help me begin to separate my life from Gene's, there remained situations where I couldn't get away because our parents were best friends. That meant since we weren't yet old enough to drive, we were still carpooling together.

When we were both freshmen, my sister drove us to and from school every day at the beginning of that year. Michelle was not afraid of Gene like I was. She fought back verbally and stood up to him if necessary.

Michelle thoroughly enjoyed listening to her music in the car whenever she drove us anywhere. "I love this song! This is my jam." She turned the dial to the right as usual.

I put my hand on my head, bracing for it.

"Ba, ba, mmm… yeah . . ." She started to warm up to the beat. Her hands tapped on the steering wheel.

"Oh my gosh. I hate this song. It sucks so bad." Gene tried to ruin her moment. "How do you even like this kind of music?" He curled his lip in disgust.

Without skipping a beat, Michelle stretched for the dial one more time, but this time, she cranked that puppy as far as it could go until our eardrums were about to explode.

My ears might have been screaming for mercy, but I was smiling on the inside. I always envied her strength to do things like this. I wanted to be able to stand up for myself too.

All Gene could do was suffer in the backseat with his hands over his ears because Michelle wasn't going to budge if he challenged her. However, one day, he did.

It was another typical day when we were riding home from school, but this time, the music wasn't blaring through the speakers.

The main noise to hear on this day was Gene's voice, which included many opinions about various people or things.

"Dude, can you believe the lunch lady got mad today about one bag of chips?" Gene started to look for my response which wasn't going to happen anymore. This was my big decision, and I needed to stay firm with it. I was no longer going to react even though I had things I wanted to say.

You weren't supposed to take them anyway.

He continued talking to himself. "She totally overreacted. Did you see her face? I should've reached over and snatched that hair net off her head."

Yes. She was mad because you did something you weren't supposed to do.

"It was just like that time your dad got mad when I took one extra party favor at your birthday. He was all worked up for no reason. That was so dumb." Gene believed his own lies.

I realized he suddenly was targeting my dad, and I should have said something right then, but I was trying to remain true to my stance on not acknowledging his words. Even doing that was a huge step for me.

By this moment, we had already driven about thirty minutes, and we were almost to Gene's house to drop him off. He continued making some harsh comments about my dad, but I don't remember all of them.

Michelle was fuming. "If you keep making fun of my dad, I'm going to kick you out of this car." Her eyebrows were rigid and her face was turning red.

Gene laughed. "Yeah right. Whatever."

"I will stop this car right now!" Michelle yelled.

Because we were about to pull onto his street, he stirred the pot. "Okay." He smirked and shook his head in disbelief.

Suddenly, Michelle stopped the car at the top of the street and shouted, "Get out!"

He said, "No," and laughed again.

She roared louder. "I said get out!"

"No."

"Get out of this car, right now!"

"No," he chuckled. He wasn't backing down this time.

She spun the tires and sped up to his house before slamming on the brakes. Gene got out of the car.

"I hate him!" Michelle exclaimed. "How do you deal with him every single day?"

I shrugged my shoulders because I didn't know how to explain myself, but she knew I was on her side. We rode the rest of the way home in silence but with a mutual understanding of one another.

This event was the perfect example showing how Gene didn't care about other people's feelings. If he made someone feel bad, it didn't matter. This was his way of life.

My sister was probably one of the only people to ever try and stand up to him. Most of the others were like I had been in that they reaffirmed his words or actions with a chuckle like his. However, Michelle did not like him at all, and she didn't care if anyone knew. Gene just wasn't used to people like my sister testing his ways, but I wished it had opened his eyes a little more.

Many events happened very early on in our freshman year. It was possible my decision to not reaffirm Gene anymore had a negative effect. When he was making fun of my dad in the car, I wasn't reaffirming him. I was just letting him talk until my sister couldn't take it any longer. I guess one might argue I was encouraging his words by saying nothing; however, it was a giant step for me to keep my mouth closed and not to give him that reassuring chuckle I had done for so long.

How was I able to remain strong in my efforts with this and not relapse? I relied heavily on the other world in which I was living—tennis.

CHAPTER 13

I had progressed in my tennis skills immensely in a very short period of time. By the following year, I was already at the highest level of tournament play, and I was right up there in the mix with the best players at the Academy and in the state.

The next event was a major turning point for some reason, and I still don't know why.

It was fall break, but all of the public schools were still in session. It was basically only the private-school kids. We had nothing to do over the week off because I still couldn't drive, and all the other tennis players were in school during the day. So one morning I asked Phillip, the only tennis friend who went to my school and also played at the Academy, if he would meet me at the tennis courts to hit. He obliged and met me up there.

This place was my safe haven, and nothing could have been more perfect than to capitalize on the amazing weather this day had to offer us. The sun was shining with just a few clouds in the sky. A few autumn leaves were floating to the ground in the slow wisps of wind. We popped open a fresh can of tennis balls and started to rally back and forth.

POP! Thud.

"I'm so glad we don't have school today," Phillip grunted as he hit the ball.

POP! Thud.

"Amen to that," I agreed.

Phillip didn't understand how strong my amen really was though because he didn't know what I was going through. I was so thankful I had a place like this where I could get away.

POP! Whoosh!

"Oops. Let me get that." I hit one into the net.

I casually walked toward the ball as it slowly rolled off the bottom lip of the net and headed toward my feet. With my racquet in one hand, I pinned the ball against the side of my shoe and lifted until I let go, allowing the ball to bounce once on the ground, then once more with my racquet, and finally back into my hand.

"Here you go," I fed the ball in.

POP! Thud.

"Huhhhhhh!" Phillip grunted again.

A bit more inaudibly than him, I breathed out as I hit it back.

"Hiyaaaaa!" Phillip squealed and tried to rip the ball as hard as he could.

I smiled and let Phillip be himself because that was what I loved about being here. Nowhere else in the world offered this to me.

While we were hitting, a sudden breeze blew across the court and caused me to frame the ball, accidentally sailing it over Phillip's head into the back fence.

CLANK!

"Oh, dang!" Phillip grinned.

"Oops again." I couldn't help but chuckle.

We were having a hard time not laughing. Phillip's noisy antics were making both of us bend over and hold our stomachs.

"You were like hiiiyaaaaa!!!" I hunched over grabbing my side.

"I know. I know." Phillip shrugged and smiled.

"Alright, let's keep hitting. We do have that tournament coming up soon, you know," I reminded him.

ZzzzzzzzzzzzzzzzzzzzzzzzZZZZzzzzzz

Phillip looked over his shoulder. "Do you hear that?"

Our fun was suddenly halted by the loud sound of high-pitched Go-Ped engines buzzing into the parking lot.

No way.

It was Gene, Jackson, and Crews.

"Here you go." I quickly fed the next ball in so Phillip couldn't ask questions. I put my blinders back on and only allowed myself to look at the ball. Everything around me became blurry except for the bright yellow tennis ball. I was so zoned in I could see the letters of the imprinted logo with each rotation. My strings gripped the ball each time and created a force of topspin that carried the ball in a perfect arching motion across the net. My heart was beating in my temples, but my breathing was pushing out the fear. There was no way I was going to miss a shot right now.

Even though I tried not to look at them, I could see their silhouettes approach the fence.

"Tyler! What's up?" barked Crews.

"What are you doing? Can we play?" Jackson was trying to get a reaction. Their shoulders were hiccupping up and down as they snickered.

One thing tennis taught me was to stay in the moment, one point at a time, and to keep my emotions in check because in tennis, it's me against the world, and I have to solve my own problems. Tennis is one of the few sports where on-court coaching during a match isn't allowed, and the players have to experience the ups and downs of a match by themselves, and they have to overcome adversity alone. In addition to that, there is no clock ticking to let you know when everything is finished. So if things aren't going well, but you keep your composure and don't give up, there's always a chance to come back victorious in the end.

I repetitively hit the ball over and over again as I honed in on practicing my patience.

"Tennis sucks!" Gene shouted through the fence.

"Yeah! Look how gay they look," Crews added.

I tried blocking them out with every other sound possible. POP! Thud. Squeak.

But they countered every POP with a whip of their own.

"You suck!" Each of them shouted between shots hoping we would miss.

Phillip kept looking at me like *what is going on*, but he somehow knew I wanted him to keep hitting and not say a word.

If I reacted, they won, so I continued to ignore them. This was the practice I had put into place of not acknowledging Gene. I was in the mode of giving the silent treatment, and they did not like that.

"Oh, you think you are so cool, don't you?" Jackson yelled.

"Oh yeah?" Crews poked.

"Well, *@#% you!" Gene leaned into the fence.

They walked back to their Go-Peds and revved the engines. "Yeah! *@#% you!"

ZZZZZzzzzzzzzzzzzzzzzzzzzzzzzzzzzzz...

And then they were gone.

I know this may sound crazy after all I have told you, but this was the first time any of the negative comments had been targeted directly at me in a major way. My whole life, I was mainly an observer and listener to all of this. Now I was a true victim.

Phillip and I finally stopped to get some water, and he looked at me. "What was that?"

I tried my best to explain to him, but who would understand a long story like that? I looked him in the eye and with a straight face said, "That's just how they are. Don't worry about it."

"Don't worry about it?" Phillip tilted his head.

"Trust me. It's fine." I assured him.

"They were cursing you out! Do you know those guys?"

"Yeah. They go to our school. Phillip, it's okay. Let's get back to hitting." I brushed it off. In my heart, I had won because I didn't snap back at them. I kept my cool, like a true tennis player.

"Whatever, Tyler. If you say so." Phillip shrugged.

We resumed our spots across the net from one another. For a while, neither of us made a sound or spoke. Only the racquet, the ball, and our shoes did the talking.

POP! Thud.

Squeak! POP! Thud.

I'm not sure if Gene needed this explosion before moving on, but the final attack on me seemed to help us take a step forward. He started to leave me alone. Maybe he was finally taking notice of my blinders and how serious I was about blocking him out.

CHAPTER 14

From that tennis blowup onward, I felt there was a marked separation from Gene, even though I had class with him. I had finally come to a point where I sat in a completely different area than him in the classroom. I was no longer going over to spend the night at his home. My parents still spent time with his parents, but I was never present. Tennis was my out. I spent so much time at the Academy that it took up all of my free time.

My mind and emotions were at a point where I hated being at school, and I loved being at tennis. At school, I had missed the opportunity to gain friends at the beginning of freshman year because I was so immersed in figuring out how to dissociate myself from Gene. Now I had created an even larger wall between myself and everyone there because I was not attending any school-related social events.

On the other hand, at tennis, everybody was my friend, and everyone was a friend to everyone. I'm talking approximately forty kids daily from ages ten to eighteen years old. It didn't matter how old anyone was.

My favorite game was called "Around the World," where all forty kids were on one tennis court together at the same time.

Stacy shouted, "I need everyone from Tyler all the way over to Campbell on the baseline to my left in one line!" She held out her hand and fanned it toward the back fence in the direction she wanted us to go.

All twenty or so kids ran to jockey for their place in line. Boys and girls from lower middle school all the way up to seniors in high school were all smiling and ready to have some fun.

"Okay! Now, I need Peyton, Phillip, and everyone else to head to the other baseline on the opposite side! Everyone has two lives. Every time you hit your shot over the net, you must run around the right net post and get in the end of the line on the other side of the net, hence why they call it 'Around the World.' If you miss a shot, you lose a life. When you are out of lives, you are out of the game, and you need to sit next to the side fence until we have a champion."

The funny thing about this game was the world was separated into two halves, but I loved both sides of this world. After I hit the ball, I left one set of friends and went to rejoin the others, but I could still see everyone smiling no matter which half I was standing with.

"Here we go! Ball in! Coming to ya, Campbell!" Stacy fed the first ball.

POP! Squeak.

Campbell immediately dashed to the other side of the net while his ball flew midair toward Peyton.

Thud.

"Woohoo!" Campbell hollered.

POP! Whoosh.

"Noooo!" Peyton's shot went straight into the net. "Can I keep my life, Stacy? Campbell was making noise!" He tried to present his argument but couldn't hide the huge grin on his face.

"That's a life!" Stacy laughed. "Go get in the other line, Peyton! There's lots of noise in tennis. We have to learn to deal with it. Next ball coming to ya, Tyler! Here it is."

With my tongue stuck out to the side, I turned my shoulders and leaned into the shot.

POP! Thud.

I raced to the other side, not looking at my shot.

"Whoa! Tyler!" Stacy shouted. "Right in the corner! That's a winner. Sorry, Phillip. That's a life lost. Head to the other side."

Phillip lowered his brow, pointed two fingers at his eyes, and then turned them around toward me but spit out a laugh as he tried to keep a poker face.

The fun continued for everyone in this way for at least ten minutes until many people, including myself, had lost both lives. The playing field had dwindled down to only two, Campbell and Maria, but she was only eleven years old. Campbell was seventeen and an amazing player.

"You got this, Maria! Woohoo!" Peyton cheered from the sideline.

Campbell lifted the left side of his mouth and got into his ready position.

"You are amazing, Maria! We believe in you!" Phillip belted out.

"We love you too, Campbell," Peyton added, "but Maria will be the champion!" He giggled.

Stacy gave the final instructions. "Since this is the championship round, once you hit the ball, do not run to the other side. Instead, spin one time in a circle and get ready for the next shot. And to the crowd, no yelling anything during the point. Here we go. Ball in."

Stacy fed the ball to Campbell.

POP! Thud.

He zoomed into a 360-degree revolution, causing his hat to fly off and land on the ground. "Ahh! My lucky hat!" He grabbed his head with one of his hands but quickly prepared for the next ball.

"Hiiiiya!" Maria roared from within her tiny frame.

POP! Thud.

Sweet little Maria sent that ball flying right back over the net and spun in a circle like a ballerina with her tennis skirt flaring outward and her pigtails flailing like a helicopter.

Campbell took one step to his left to get into position for the incoming ball but accidentally stepped on his hat as he took his swing.

"Ahh!" He stumbled just enough.

Whiff!

"Noooo!" cried Campbell with a smile on his face and his hands on his head.

"Maria! Champion of the world!" Stacy pumped her fist. "Girls rule!"

A round of applause erupted amongst a sea of smiles.

Maria grabbed the sides of her skirt with the tips of her fingers and curtsied as she put her right toe to the ground behind her left leg.

"Maria!" Campbell picked up his hat and jogged toward the net. "You rock, sister!" Then he gave her a big high five.

Peyton went over and held out his hand. "Maria! You are the bomb dot com! Get it!"

POP!

This time, that sound wasn't the racquet hitting the ball, but rather pure joy resonating right out of Maria's hand onto Peyton's.

"Youch!" He winced, then he turned around. "Campbell, you are still the best. You know we love you. Plus, you won the other hundred times we've played this game."

"It's cool," he replied and cupped his right hand and held it up for Peyton to meet him halfway.

Peyton reached over the net as their two palms met creating the slightest echo. This was the sound of mutual respect and understanding of true friends.

"Hey, you guys want to come over to my house after tennis for some video games and a movie?" Peyton was soliciting his invitation to anyone who was able to come.

I ended up hitching a ride with Peyton. When we arrived at his house, we pulled around back to park in the garage. I noticed he had a perfectly flat driveway with a basketball hoop glistening in the sun.

"Alright! Here we are!" He put the car in park. "Welcome to my humble abode. Come on. Let me show you inside."

CREAK.

"Mom! We're home! Is it okay if a few friends come over? We will totally leave you in peace." He reached his arms around his mom before she could respond. "I love you, Mom!" Then he looked at her with puppy-dog eyes.

She couldn't help but let out the funniest little laugh. "I love you too, Peyton. Of course."

His mom turned to me. "Tyler! How are you? I'm so glad you could come. Peyton has told me all about you. Please, make yourself at home."

I learned quickly this was the norm at their house, with tennis players showing up to enjoy time together off the court.

DING-DONG!

Peyton rolled his eyes as he opened the glass door. "Campbell, you know you don't have to ring the doorbell. Just come on in. You know the drill." He patted him on the back as he passed the doorway.

HONK-HONK!

Before he shut the door, more pulled up to the house and came trickling inside, even Maria and her older brother. There were other sets of siblings. Then Easton arrived. He was another newbie to the group but not to tennis. He was becoming one of my good friends because everyone else had been friends together for so long. We sort of gravitated toward each other at times.

A mixture of ages had shown up to the house now, but the vibe was more like a youth group. The older kids acted like bigger brothers and sisters to the younger ones. We all took care of one another.

We all made our way into the game and movie room. "Guys, who wants to play the newest tactical shooting game on the market? But it's not gruesome. It's not that kind of game. They say it's okay for ages ten and up. I just got it yesterday, and I have four controllers." Peyton raised his eyebrows to see who reacted first.

"I'm in!" shouted Campbell.

"Easton? You want in?" Peyton asked.

"Sure." He reached his hand out to take the controller.

"Awesome. We need one more. Tyler? Can you be our fourth?" Peyton requested.

I hesitated. "Ummm." I didn't like these types of games, and I had grown comfortable enough with my new group of friends not to be fake about how I felt. "I think I am going to shoot basketball in the driveway while y'all play, if that's okay."

"By yourself?" Peyton was surprised. "I mean, if you want."

Fairly confidently I responded, "Yeah. And anyone else who ends up wanting to. Someone else can have my spot for the game though."

"Okay. Cool. Yeah. There are a few basketballs in a small basket to the left of where I parked my car. They're all yours!" Instead of trying to make me feel guilty, he said, "I feel bad though, so let me know if you want to play the game or end up wanting us to come outside."

"Sounds good. No worries." I knew right then these were my best friends in the world. I declared my own opinion about something, and I wasn't ridiculed for it. Shooting free throws and three-point heaves, I spent an hour outside, but I was as happy as could be. I heard muffled reactions to the video game through the back door.

"Oooooooo!!!"

"Ahhhh!!"

"HAHAHA!!"

CREAK.

"Hey! Tyler! Are you good out here?" Campbell called out. "We're stopping to eat something before watching a movie. You want to come in?"

"Sure!" I was starving.

After we all grabbed a quick bite, they all came outside to shoot basketball with me instead. Easton and Campbell grabbed two extra basketballs.

I parked myself near the edge of the driveway for my specialty, the corner three.

"Check this!" Easton tossed up a mid-range jumper.

CLANK!

It bounced off the rim and headed toward me. With one basketball already in my right hand, I held out my left to cradle the second as it landed softly in my giant mitts.

"Oh. Nice catch, Tyler." Easton clapped his hands. "I thought I was going to have to chase that ball down the alleyway."

"Easton, this is how it's done." Campbell bent his knees, threw up a free throw, and held his hand out like a bird's beak.

CLANK!

His shot hit the left side of the rim and was sailing my direction again. It took a giant bounce off the ground twice as tall as me. Looking up where I could see the clouds behind the falling ball, I did not instinctively think to pass the two other basketballs away so I could catch the incoming cannonball. Instead, as soon as the ball dropped low enough, I tossed the ball from my right hand diagonally up and to the left, catching Campbell's shot in my right. From there, I started juggling all three basketballs for only about eight tosses before sending two right back over to Easton and Campbell.

"Holy moly! Tyler!" Peyton exclaimed. "That was incredible! I knew you could juggle tennis balls. But basketballs? Dang. You are the most talented person I know. You have barely been playing tennis, but you already play with us. Your basketball skills make us look like we aren't athletic. And you can juggle like that!"

I shrugged my shoulders and shot my corner three.

SWOOSH!

Nothing but net. Peyton smiled at me.

We all hung outside long enough to forget about ever watching a movie. I was having a blast. This was the type of situation I could juggle with my eyes closed. Everything was right with this group. There was never a worry about anything.

On the other hand, back in the school world, I hid in plain sight. I started to grow my hair out so I could hide behind it. I walked the halls with my head down, and even if somebody tried to say "hello" to me, many times I ignored them and kept walking.

I hated feeling stuck. I didn't fit in at all. I was not part of any group at school. Even though I was on the tennis team there, Phillip and I were at a certain level of tennis where our coach let us go to our serious practices at the Academy four of the five days a week, so we were only required to be at a school practice on campus once a week.

At the Academy clinics, I didn't feel like I had to hide at all. People put me in the category of a funny person who made them laugh, and they enjoyed being around me. We were all experiencing the grind of a serious and strict tennis regimen together daily, and it brought us closer as friends.

Experiencing depression at school for eight hours a day followed by two hours of bliss at tennis played with my emotions. As I progressed further with my skills, tennis got more and more competitive, and it became more about the achievements than the experience, or at least it was starting to feel that way when I realized all my friends were having greater success.

We were having so much fun traveling together once a month to different cities to play high-level tournaments. In the tournaments, if I lost my first match, I got put in the consolation bracket, and if I lost again, I was done. Basically, I was guaranteed two matches, but if I performed well, I could play as many as five.

I started comparing myself to everyone else when I played because it was an independent sport, for the most part. Players got ranked within their state or region. As time went on, the rankings shifted. Campbell, Phillip, and Easton kept climbing, but I remained stagnant. I didn't have the same natural fight my friends had when it came to being competitive. Much of that came from being around Gene and his friends caring so much about winning that I didn't care as much, and it hindered my tennis performance.

As we continued traveling to tournaments, my record was slipping. When we were about fifteen years old, Phillip and Easton were in the top twenty in the state. Campbell was in the top ten. The majority of everyone else was in the top forty to fifty or better. I was closer to one hundred.

I started to compare myself to them, and I told myself I couldn't do it. I stopped caring, and that seeped over into other areas of my life.

By my junior year in high school, during the second quarter, I learned I was receiving three Ds on my report card, but it hadn't yet arrived at our house. I had never gotten worse than one C as a final grade in my entire life. For this to happen truly showed how I was being affected.

I had the mindset of, "Well, I'm going to be a senior anyway, so who cares?" At tennis tournaments, I was losing my first match and my second. Eventually, my record was two and twenty-eight. That meant two wins and twenty-eight losses. My friends' records were closer to twenty and ten or better. They definitely had more wins than losses.

I didn't care anymore. I was in a depression from school as well as from not experiencing success in tennis at the highest level, but the one thing I still had going for me was the friendships. Phillip, Easton, and Campbell wanted me to succeed and tried to give me advice.

We had finished practice one day, and Phillip came and sat next to me on the steps up to the pro shop.

"You ready for the big tournament tomorrow?"

"It doesn't really matter. I'm just going to lose." I hung my head. "I mean, I want to win. I know y'all get bored watching me lose all the time."

"Tyler, we don't think like that. Don't worry about what we are thinking while you're out there." Phillip tried to encourage me. "Going into tomorrow, why don't you just do it for yourself? Don't do it for us or for anybody else." He patted me on the shoulder.

"Okay." I lifted my head. "I'll try."

I've never done much for myself. I have been programmed to make others happy. It has never been about what I wanted. How do I even operate in that way?

When I got to the tournament the next day, my attitude wasn't fully right, and I lost. Overcoming adversity in a tennis match was a major obstacle, and I didn't have the fight to get back in it. So once I was down, I was down, and there was no climbing back out of it. If I was ever matched up against a friend in a tournament, game over. There was no way I was going to try and beat a friend. I don't know why, but that's just how it was for me.

The depression coming from tennis got to a point where all I cared about anymore was being around my friends. I couldn't lose these friendships because I had never had any like them before in my life. Therefore, I continued to travel to these tournaments from month to month, but I was losing ninety-nine percent of the time.

My report card came in over Christmas break, and I wasn't at home when it arrived in the mail.

When I got home from Peyton's house one day, my parents were waiting for me in the kitchen. The light was shining down from above my parents, casting shadows on the floor. I had grown just above six feet tall, but I felt extremely small at this moment. My dad's arms were crossed, and my mom was glaring over her glasses with the report card in hand.

"What... is... this?!" She began the interrogation.

I don't recall getting any words in the conversation. My parents vented their anger and frustration as they well should have and had the right to.

"We don't understand. We can't think of a reason for this. We don't really know what you do all the time when you are over at Peyton's house with all your friends. You're always gone."

"What?" I squinted in confusion.

I shoot basketball and watch movies. Sometimes I reluctantly play video games. I am living in a dream with the best friends in the world. What is wrong with that?

Before I could say anything, she added, "You don't tell us what you do while you hang out. For all we know, you could be on drugs. You've grown your hair out so long. Are you on drugs?!"

"No," I said as I calmly chuckled in disbelief. Explaining myself seemed unnecessary, yet my stomach was now in my chest. Not only did I have these awful grades against me, but now I had the added drug assumption. As a slow processor, I had no idea how to defend myself. I thought my character was good enough.

Here I was, a junior in high school, who now based my whole life on not being like Gene or being around people like him. I was never at any parties that had drinking or drugs. In the tennis world, nobody did that because we were playing at such a high level there was no time for things like that. I did not have a typical high school experience of partying late into the night. And here I was with my parents wanting to know if I was on drugs.

The pit in my stomach transitioned to a heatwave in my head because I knew in my heart that I was a good person, and I was being accused of doing something that wouldn't fall under that category. I knew I had no right to get three Ds, and I shouldn't use the excuse of anger and depression, but that's what it was. I started to shut down even more because my parents didn't trust me. I couldn't erase the memory of them wondering if I was somebody who took drugs, when on the contrary, I should have been praised for never having gone to a single party to this point in my whole high school career, and I had not once had a drink of alcohol or tried marijuana like many of the other people I knew. When I was at Peyton's house, it was simple fellowship as usual.

My mom continued, "Not only that, but you have had an awful attitude at tennis. It has been so frustrating because I pay thousands of dollars a month for us to be members at the Academy. Not to mention all of the weekly private lessons I cover as well. Then there's the tournament fees and travel expenses for flights and hotels. It all adds up. And for you to be acting the way you have on the court is unacceptable. What I've been hearing from your coaches is you aren't even trying. Each tournament you are losing and losing. Why am I paying for all of this if that's the type of effort you're going to put in?" She threw her hands in the air.

My head had cooled down, but my heart was now sinking in my chest.

She looked back at the report card. "I'll tell you what. This is the final straw."

I was near ready to quit tennis anyhow except for not wanting to lose my friends. The next tournament over Christmas break was in our hometown.

A tear rolled down her cheek. "I've already paid for the next tournament, and you better believe I'm coming to watch. If I witness you not giving full competitive effort to your opponent through the duration of your matches, then I hate to say this, but I will no longer pay for tennis. That means you'll have to take some time away from the game." She wiped under her eyes with her index finger. My dad hadn't moved, still in his supportive-stance position, looking down, sending the same message in a silent way.

To see my mom give me the look of helplessness hurt because I never intended on putting any of my own pain onto her, but that is what it came to in the end. I knew I was in trouble, but in the heat of the moment, part of me didn't care if I was going to have to quit tennis.

"Yes, ma'am," I nodded. There was no way I was going to present an argument.

I walked away with the pit back in my stomach because of the unknown future ahead of me. I wondered if I was going to have to say goodbye to everyone. Flashes of smiles and moments of true community circled in my mind: Peyton's compliments, Campbell's support, Phillip's encouragement, Easton's new friendship. My heart knew what it wanted, but it didn't know if it would be able to get over the hump that had been standing in my way at every tournament.

About a week later, I had my first-round match. My mom came as planned. She parked herself right outside the fence in her picnic-style lawn chair and didn't move a muscle. Praise the Lord, I was playing against somebody ranked lower than me. The thud of the tennis ball hitting the ground wasn't enough to drown out the pounding thud of my heartbeat inside my chest and temples. In the end, my skill level outmatched the other boy's, and I won despite all the nerves. My mom was proud of me. "See. I knew you could do it. Why don't you do that every time?"

At first I thought she meant to win, but she was referring to my effort.

"Most things in life don't come easy, and obstacles will get in your way, but you have to keep moving forward with your chin up. I feel like you did that today, and maybe you didn't really have to come back from behind to win. You were sort of up the whole time, but even when things didn't go your way, you kept it together. There's a lot to juggle in this world, including your own emotions and reactions to unexpected adversity, and you have to figure out ways to block out the noise so you can reach your goals. Like this—catch!" She quickly tossed a tennis ball above my head. I leaned out of the way and let it slowly float into the palm of my hand. "Good job today, Tyler. I love you." And she gave me a kiss on the cheek.

I felt like a weight had been lifted off my shoulders.

A few hours later, there was my second-round match. Mom watched from a distance this time inside her car in the parking lot. I still gave full effort, and I played okay, but I got demolished. I only won two games, and in tennis, that is not a lot. The astonishing part about it all was after the match.

I went to the net to shake my opponent's hand, and the boy said, "Hey, would you possibly want to be my doubles partner if they let you sign up with me? I know the registration deadline has already passed, but the doubles partner I always play with had a mental breakdown last week and quit tennis."

Ha! That should have been me!

He then proceeded to say, "I mean, you have a really good serve and great volleys. Do you think you would want to play if they'll let you pay the doubles fee and take my original partner's place?"

Even though I knew she couldn't hear, I glanced over my shoulder to see if my mom was listening. As you can imagine, I was flattered and a little excited someone wanted me on their team, but I was very hesitant to ask Mom to pay another fee after our recent conversation.

Shortly after, we grabbed our bags, and my mom met us over at the tournament desk where we turned in our score.

Unsure how she felt about my performance, I hung my head slightly, but then she put her arm on my back. "Good match, Tyler." She knew I had lost but also saw I truly tried my best. It just didn't go my way.

"Thanks, Mom. So… ummm… " I fumbled to find the right words.

"What is it, Tyler?" my mom asked.

"This is Jimmy," I said as he stepped away from the desk.

"Hi, Mrs. Richardson. It's nice to meet you." He was very outgoing. "Did Tyler tell you about . . ."

She looked at me with one eyebrow raised. "Tell me about what?"

"Well, Mom," I jumped in, "Jimmy wants to know if I can play doubles with him this weekend."

"Yeah," Jimmy added. "I asked at the desk, and they said it was okay as long as you were able to pay the fees right now."

I tried not to make eye contact with Mom while she pondered this because I had already put her through enough. I expected a quick "No."

"Sure," she replied. "No problem at all." She reached into her purse, pulled out her wallet, and wrote a check on the spot.

So I signed up with my new, temporary partner, Jimmy. He was unlike anybody I had ever played doubles with before because he had so much knowledge to share about how to win. It was like having a coach on the court at the same time with me. To make things even better, he made me laugh the whole time we played, which helped reduce any mental pressure I typically put on myself.

Ready to attack, I bent low near the net waiting for the right moment.

POP! Whoosh.

"Ugh . . ." I dumped an easy put-away shot right into the net. I rolled my eyes. "Sorry, Jimmy."

"Dude," he looked me in the eye, "you are an animal up there. Do it again! Rawwwrrrr!" He threw his hand out like a tiger claw.

"Uhh, okay." I grinned. He helped me believe I was good and had the ability to do what he needed me to do.

The very next point, I patiently waited to hunt down the right ball again. When that moment came, I lunged for it . . .

POP!

"Booooooooom!" Jimmy yelled. "Rawwwwrrr!" He showed all his teeth like he was a wild animal.

I smiled back at him.

"What did I tell you? Keep being yourself up there at the net. I need you every time looking just like that."

Before it was my time to return the opponent's serve, he walked up to me. "Look over my shoulder. Do you see where the net player is standing? He doesn't even think you will hit it his direction. Look at the land he is leaving open for you to claim with a down-the-line laser, but you don't even need to hit it that hard."

I nodded. Jimmy went to his position on the court. Here came the serve. My shoulders turned, I lined up my shot, and without feeling any pressure, guided the ball right past the net player who didn't even react.

Jimmy made eye contact with me and sent a funny wink my direction. He was right again.

Later in the match, when it was my time to serve, the trend continued.

We talked for a brief moment before each point to communicate our plan. It was more Jimmy talking and me listening, but I was good at that.

"Alright. Your serve is so good, Tyler. On this one, let's give 'em the spicy slice-and-dice out wide." He gave me a fist bump, and I nodded in accordance with a bit of a tilted head thinking about the word spicy and trying not to smile.

I knew exactly what he wanted me to do and how to do it. I leaned forward with all the weight on my left leg and bounced the ball three times.

Thud. Thud. Thud.

My eyes looked over the net without giving away my destination. I slowly rocked back with the weight now on my right leg, tossed the ball into the air as my left hip immediately leaned back the other way, shifting my weight once again to the front. Time stood still for a moment while my left arm pointed to the sky and the rest of my body was in the tennis trophy position. The ball floated in the air slightly above my head and over my right shoulder. Then somebody hit the fast-forward button.

POP! Zing!

My racquet cut the right, outside edge of the ball, sending it into a perfect spinning, curving frenzy to the left.

"Ace! Boom-shocka-locka!" Jimmy pumped his fist and skipped back toward me to talk about the next serve. "That was sick nasty." He gave me a slight nudge on the shoulder with his fist. "You are unstoppable."

"Okay, so what do you want me to do with this next one?" I asked.

"Oh man. Let's send 'em the Tyler special. Give 'em the T-Bone T-Bomb right down the middle of the court." He held out his pinky.

"What's that for?" I was befuddled.

"Pinky promise." He kept the straightest face.

I burst out laughing as we shook pinkies.

"Here we go." He danced off to his spot.

I repeated my service routine, and . . .

BAM!

I sent that ball whistling right where he had directed me, and we won the point again. Jimmy was making me so relaxed out there. I didn't even realize we were running away with the match. I was laughing more than I was thinking about messing up, and that was odd because my mind had grown so accustomed to losing and shutting down, but Jimmy somehow understood what I needed to hear.

Winning points turned into winning games, which then became sets. Before I knew it we were shaking hands with our opponents, and we had won.

We won our first match.

Then we won our second match.

And our third match.

And then, we won the finals!

What? How did this happen? We won the whole thing!

Not only did we bring home the trophy, but we had beaten people who were ranked very high in singles. I'm talking about players who were in the top twenty and top ten in the state!

There was even a write-up in the newspaper the following week about our successful run.

It was like a slow-motion dream. I was back and part of a new and improved doubles team! We signed up for the January tournament together. We won the January tournament. We signed up for the February tournament. We at least got to the finals or won it. Same thing in March. Same thing in April. Same thing in May. Same thing in June! By July, in the biggest tournament of the year, they had a news clip of us winning our semifinals match on television! We ended up losing in the finals to the highest ranked team, but we were considered to be the second-ranked doubles team in the entire state for the sixteen-year-old division. In my heart, we were really number one because the team that beat us in the finals had only won about eight matches total that year without losing any, but Jimmy and I had won about twenty-five doubles matches and only lost about two or three.

Even though I still struggled in singles, the doubles success gave me a new winning attitude. I still had some depression about singles when I compared myself to my friends, but then it all got balanced out when I beat them or the highest ranked players from singles in the doubles world. What a strange turn of events, to go from one of the lowest ranked members in singles to one of the highest ranked doubles teams in the state.

Eventually, we traveled to play my first National Open Tennis Tournament held in a neighboring state. On this trip, it was me, Jimmy, Phillip, Easton, and one of our coaches. I was the only one without any experience on the national level. Everyone here looked the part with name brand tennis clothing, shoes, hats, and really nice racquet bags that held up to six racquets or more. This was serious, but I did my best to blend in with some of the same gear. Jimmy couldn't have cared less, but it was this type of fun, pressure-free attitude that helped me raise my game.

The tournament started with all of the singles matches first. Despite my greatest efforts, I lost my first and second match. Phillip had a nail-biter with the number one seed in the opening round and almost beat him but came up just short. Jimmy and Easton both came out victorious in their first-round matches.

The doubles began during the first evening. The sun was beginning to set, but not quite low enough to turn on the lights for the courts. Phillip and Easton had been doubles partners for a while now, but Easton and I had become best friends, and we always talked with each other about how we wanted to eventually be a doubles team one day and turn professional. This was a tough topic to discuss because I was winning so much with

Jimmy, and Easton had struggled a little bit with Phillip in some of the tournaments we played.

"You got this, Easton! Let's go, Phillip!" I cheered them on while Jimmy and I waited to be called for our first match.

Things started slow after getting down early, but Jimmy tried to settle them down with, "Spicy noodles!" CLAP! CLAP! CLAP! "I love you, Phillip!"

Unfortunately, Easton and Phillip were both already past their frustration level. No smiles resulted, so Jimmy held off.

"Jimmy and Tyler!" An announcement came through a megaphone. "Jimmy and Tyler! Please report to the tournament desk."

"That's us, big guy." Jimmy shouldered me to get up.

I sat lingering for a moment watching Phillip and Easton because I wanted them to win, but it wasn't looking hopeful. Their shoulders already sagged and the communication was lacking. Jimmy made me snap out of it when he tossed my giant tennis bag at me. He walked off, but I jogged to catch up with him. We went to the desk and got a new can of tennis balls for our match.

"Tyler, check this out." Jimmy grabbed two tennis racquets from his large bag and left it on the grass. Then he pulled out two single racquet cases, slipped one racquet into each one, and zipped them shut. Both cases had a carrying strap on them. "Help me out for a second, boss man." He looped one strap over his shoulder like a guitar, and he was trying to cross the other one over his other shoulder, but it was getting stuck.

I was already laughing. "Here you go." I quickly fed the strap through so both racquets made an X on his back.

It was honestly hilarious because everyone else here kept their game faces on and carried around their top-of-the-line tennis bags. Jimmy was trying to make us look like scrubs walking out to the court.

"Gracias, mijo." Then he bent down and pulled his socks as high as he could. "Let's do this."

We made our way out to the court for our match.

POP! Ssssssss . . .

We opened the fresh can of tennis balls.

Jimmy spoke in a high-pitched voice. "Hi! I'm Jimmy, and this is Tyler. This tournament is top-notch with so many amazing players." He was acting like this whole scene was new to him as he uncrossed his racquet straps and grunted.

Our opponents looked at each other when Jimmy turned his back, and they both raised their eyebrows, shook their heads, and fist bumped. After seeing Jimmy's singular racquet cases and listening to his introduction, they believed they had this one in the bag.

After we warmed up for a few minutes, Jimmy called out in his squeaky voice again, "Are you guys ready to warm up serves?"

They nodded in agreement.

Out of the corner of my eye, I could tell Jimmy was doing something odd. I turned my head and witnessed Jimmy going through the most unorthodox service motion I had ever seen and sending the ball over like a rainbow at ten miles an hour. I was ready to fall on the floor laughing, but I was catching on to what he was doing. We both knew we were ready to rock these guys, but Jimmy had a few mind games for them up front.

Once everyone was ready, we all walked to the net to see who would serve first. Jimmy said, "I'll spin. Up or down?"

"Up."

Jimmy held the handle of his racquet, put the other end of it to the ground, and spun it until it fell over landing on one side. He looked down at the bottom of the handle to see if the logo indicated they had predicted correctly.

"It's down. We'll receive. Here you go." He gave them all three tennis balls.

Jimmy told me early on in our partnership how we were always going to elect to receive if we won the toss because he believed if we gave everything we had in the very first game and broke our opponents down on their very first service game, they would not be able to crawl back out of that hole. I had always listened to what he preached because it worked.

"Have a good match, guys," our opponent called out and held up the ball before his first serve.

Jimmy looked back at me before my first return of the match, winked, nodded, and turned his hat around backward. At this exact moment, I knew he was ready to turn it on and shock these guys.

POP! Thud.

The first serve of the match came sizzling in.

POP! Zing!

I hit a winner. They didn't even touch it.

Jimmy and I repeated that same action the first four points of the match, stealing the first game, and we never looked back. We won every single game except one to take a decisive victory. Our opponents never had time to know what hit 'em.

Jimmy's silly mind games combined with being unseeded in the doubles draw, nobody knew who we were and didn't seem to feel the need to worry about us. The tournament based the seedings off of singles players' rankings, so we were not identified as a threat, but we both knew what we were capable of achieving.

Winning our first match was very routine for me at this point, but I felt more accomplished because it was a national tournament.

"Nice match." Easton high fived me at the tournament desk. "You guys literally didn't miss a shot. You were like BAM-BAM-BAM!"

"Thanks, man. How did you guys end up doing?" I already knew the response.

"We lost, so we're done for the tournament since doubles is single elimination." He shook his head. "I love doubles though. I wish we could keep playing."

I felt bad for him, but I was the only one who was done with the singles part of the tournament. They all still had a shot to boost their rankings while I sat on the sideline, so I had to hang on to my doubles success.

In the following round the next day, Jimmy and I had to play the number three–seeded team. We made quick work of our foes, only giving them three games total en route to our second victory.

After the match, Phillip and Easton hopped the short side of the fence to congratulate us.

"Dude! You guys just beat the number three team in the nation!" Easton shook me by the shoulders.

"High five, man. That was insane." Phillip swung his hand into mine.

POP!

"Thanks." I remained humble, but fireworks were celebrating in my heart.

As we walked off the court, our coach was waiting for us. "Great match, you two." He gave each of us a fist bump. "Very sound playing out there today, very crisp and clean."

"Let's celebrate with some ice cream!" Jimmy joked.

"Very funny," our coach responded. "You know you have to play your next round match against the number two seed in less than an hour from now."

Oh snap.

I was starting to feel the knot in my stomach until Jimmy poked me in the tummy. "Beep-boop! Gotcha."

I flinched backward.

"Are you ready to be the biggest net monster you've ever been? You are a beast. Remember that." Jimmy somehow knew the exact moments to be serious even though he spent most of his time making us laugh.

I gave him a half smile and lifted my chin. "I got you."

"Hey, guys," Coach interjected. "Phillip and Easton still have to play singles matches tomorrow, and I don't want them baking out here in the sun all afternoon, so I am going to drop them off at the hotel, and then I will come right back to watch your match. How does that sound?"

"No problem," I said.

They each gave me and Jimmy a fist bump and then headed to the car.

What seemed like a very short time after they left, an available court opened up, and we were called for our next match. For some reason, they put us on a court far away from everyone else. This was good news for me because having all of the best players in the nation watching along the edges of the fencing during most matches was nerve-racking. Far away on our secluded court, Jimmy and I knew this was the perfect opportunity to steal another win. Nobody was worried about the number two–seeded team losing, so there wasn't a soul in sight to come check on them.

Less than thirty minutes after the first point, the wake-up call came to an end. "Good match." We shook their hands and left the court. I scanned the area for our coach, but he hadn't returned yet.

Jimmy whispered into my ear, "Tyler, when Coach pulls into the parking lot . . ."

One minute later, he parked the car, got out, and noticed we were sitting on the curb with our heads down, not talking.

"Wait a minute." He tilted his head. "You guys already played? I missed it? I'm so sorry. Don't hang your heads. Keep your chins held high. You have had a great run. You should be proud. I mean, they were the number two seed. What was the score anyway?"

Jimmy lifted his head but kept his eyes looking down. "It was eight–two." He sighed and took a deep breath before leaping into the air. "We won! Gotcha!" He wrapped his arms around Coach whose eyes were ready to pop out of his head.

"What? You did?" Coach smiled. "But I was only gone for about thirty minutes.

"We know." Jimmy gave him a soft punch on the shoulder. "We were like hello, goodbye, nice to meet you. They didn't know what hit 'em."

"Shall we call Phillip and Easton on our way to the hotel to share the good news?" Coach asked. "Or should we... ?" He threw out the idea of extending this harmless little prank. So on the drive back, he picked up the phone and called Phillip. "Hey... ya... they... well, Tyler is pretty down. We'll see you in a few... okay, bye." He hung up and turned on his evil grin. "Got 'em. Tyler, they think you are in the pits."

I knew this was all a lie, but I couldn't help but smile from ear to ear because we were going to be in the finals of a national tournament.

Jimmy shared another idea. "Tyler, when we get back to the hotel, why don't you lock yourself in the bathroom of our room. You can pretend you're so upset that you don't want to talk to anyone. Then I'll go ask Phillip and Easton for their help to come try and get you to come out."

"Okay." I was still smiling, but I only agreed because I knew this wasn't going to hurt anyone.

After we got back, we proceeded with the plan. I waited in the bathroom until—

KNOCK! KNOCK!

"Hey Tyler," Phillip said softly. "You okay?"

I didn't respond.

"It's okay, Tyler," Easton added. "Y'all still did so good."

Silence again.

The guilt started to build up inside me because Phillip and Easton had both been there for me when I needed a mental boost, and for me to try and fool them like this just didn't feel right.

I had a towel over my mouth as I tried to muffle the laughs.

"What was that noise? I heard that. I know you're in there, Tyler. Are you laughing?" Easton was suspicious, and he knew me best.

I pulled the door wide open and shouted, "Surprise! We won!"

Jimmy went from acting like he was resting to jumping up and down on the hotel bed. "Weeeeee!"

"You're lying," Phillip declared quickly, but then he looked at me, and he didn't see the same depressing glaze that always overtook me. There was true happiness in my heart.

We all joined Jimmy and started jumping on the two beds and celebrating until Coach walked in. "Okay. Okay. Guys! You're going to break the furniture. Let's celebrate at dinner instead. C'mon."

So we did. And in true Jimmy fashion, he snuck in a word with the hostess while we weren't looking. It wasn't until after we finished our meal when the whole team of waiters and waitresses came over to the table with a slice of birthday cake and a candle. They set it down in front of Coach.

"It's not my—" He tried to stop them, but they all inhaled and began to belt out the loudest rendition of "Happy Birthday" you ever heard. We were singing and laughing as we wondered what was happening.

When they finished, Coach shrugged his shoulders. "I guess I didn't have the heart to tell them they had the wrong guy."

"Actually," Jimmy snickered, "I told them it was your birthday when we walked in."

We all rolled over the edge of the table laughing and holding our stomachs.

This joyride seemed to never end, but the next day would be the cherry on top if we could pull it off.

The next morning, we were scheduled to play in the finals against the number one–seeded team, but they had to default due to catching a flight back to their home state. Honestly though,

I believe they had heard about the unseeded freight train that was screaming through the doubles draw, and they didn't want any of it. We would've beaten them anyway. Therefore, we won! I don't care what anybody says—we won a National Open doubles tournament.

Jimmy and I made it to the final of every tournament we ever played until all of a sudden, about one month later, we lost in the semifinals, and he dumped me. Just like that. In the blink of an eye, it was over.

I wonder if it was the anxiety I carried with me. Maybe it bothered him?

Things were never discussed, but it didn't matter. Jimmy had saved me, like an angel who had flown in and out to sprinkle a quick blessing of hope upon me. He had changed my life. I went from almost quitting tennis to believing in myself again. Now I was considering playing college tennis. Plus, Easton had wanted to be my doubles partner for the longest time, so we made that transition quickly, and we were pumped.

Now that we were doubles partners, we were winning like we had always envisioned. We made it to the finals of our first two tournaments, and I was still a very highly ranked doubles player. I was living the dream until one day, Easton got a girlfriend.

This created a major change in the dynamic of our friendship as well as our doubles partnership. Our time spent together outside of tennis remained similar at the beginning of their new romantic relationship, but I was now the third wheel.

Having this role left me bitter due to feeling like he didn't care about our friendship, and that he only cared about his girlfriend. I was angry, but because I spent so much of my life never having a voice, I didn't speak up to Easton about it. I figured, "Hey, if the silent treatment is my mode of solving problems, then why not try it on Easton." So I did. I tried it even though we were doubles partners still.

I gave him the silent treatment for a long enough period of a few months that when he finally tried to make amends with a very long handwritten letter, I was so closed down that I didn't accept his apology. The last tournament we ever played together was a different National Open. We were the number one–seeded team. We lost in the first round. We didn't speak to each other before the match, and we didn't speak to each other after either.

Elements of Gene always stuck with me in my mind. At times, I heard tennis players talking about one another, and sometimes people said comments like, "He thinks he is so cool. Oh my gosh. He tries to wear his hat backward and be all like, ya, what's up, I'm awesome, and you're not." This didn't happen often, but when it did, all I could think about was Gene, and it rubbed me the wrong way.

Back at the school building, if I ever passed Gene in the hallway on a free period and it was only the two of us in the hall, I put my head straight down or forward, never making eye contact. Complete separation. He didn't know anything about my tennis success, and I didn't care to know anything about his life. If I ever heard anything about him, it was from my parents who were still hanging out with his parents.

I continued to carry around a heavy, angered burden when I was at school. It was like trying to juggle bowling balls I knew I couldn't sustain. Something would eventually come crashing down.

One day we were in English class, and the teacher put up an image of an artist's painting. "Class, we are going to analyze the artist's purpose of this beautiful painting based on things we see in the image. Please take a moment to look closely at all of the different elements within the composition."

As I sat there with a separate anger about how Gene always thought about how he knew how people felt about themselves, or how tennis players knew how other tennis players thought they were cool, my insides began to boil.

Nobody on the face of this earth knows what this artist thinks or feels.

I truly believed it was imperative we speak directly to the artist if we really wanted to know, and if we didn't ask him, then we did not have the right to say anything.

Could you imagine? I couldn't even do a simple art education exercise without my mind slipping back into a deep dark place.

"Okay. Time is up." The teacher began the discussion of the painting by calling on a boy who stated why he thought the artist had included certain items in the painting, and my teapot was about to start whistling.

My hand shot up, and that never happened. I was always in the background. The teacher had to call on me because I had never raised my hand in the past.

"Thank you so much for sharing. I see Tyler's hand is raised. Go ahead." She called on me.

In a fairly angry tone, I declared, "We will never know what the artist's purpose was unless we speak with him, and I highly disagree with the first answer you just heard. It's honestly preposterous because we can't make those claims about why those items are in the painting without knowing or speaking to the artist." I huffed like I was out of breath but also like I had finished first in a track race.

I felt proud of my answer until the teacher responded in utter astonishment and anger, "Excuse me, Tyler. I am very shocked and disappointed right now. How dare you put down another student's answer in such a manner."

My face turned red from embarrassment and anger. How could she not understand my logic? This made complete sense after everything I had endured all these years.

BRRRING!

The bell rang. I bolted out of class and headed straight to the library for my free period. I grabbed a couple sheets of paper and began to write feverishly to explain myself, and this ended up turning into a description of all the things Gene had done when he spoke about people, and how I was going to make sure I would never be like him. I filled up approximately four to five sides of loose-leaf notebook paper before leaving the library that day.

The words flowed out of my fingertips like a waterfall of emotion spilling onto the paper. My pent-up anger and frustration finally had a place to land. Why had I not done this before now? It felt good to get those thoughts and feelings out of my head where they were causing so much pain and anxiety and onto paper, almost like a repository for my emotions.

I kept that paper with me for a long time. It was my constant reminder of how I wanted to live my life, or on the contrary, how I did not want to live it.

CHAPTER 15

Senior year came. I had raised my grades, but I was still at a loss. I just couldn't fathom how my school life was going, and I needed to make it to the end so I could go to college. I longed to have my own schedule and true independence away from home for the first time. Gene's shadow had followed me for many years, but I knew it couldn't last forever. There was a high chance of landing a tennis scholarship if I kept playing, and I could see a glimmer of hope along the horizon.

My one real friend at school who had been with me from the beginning was Oliver. We didn't spend every minute together, but he knew about my trials and tribulations, and he was always willing to listen to me. Oliver was really good at baseball, so we often carried a bucket of baseballs over to a nearby public diamond and had a little batting practice while we talked. He was also aware of my past fears from baseball, so he wasn't going to throw any zingers.

"So when am I ever going to get you to come to a school party?" Oliver held the bucket by its handle over his shoulder as we approached the field.

I shrugged. "Probably never? I'm sorry." I gripped the bat with my right hand and let it repetitively slap into my left palm after every few steps.

"And it's because he'll be there?" he asked.

"Oliver." I rolled my eyes. "You already know. Why are you asking? I don't want to be around that stuff. It's not a part of my life."

He responded calmly, "That's fine. You are allowed to do whatever you want. I was only checking to make sure." We finally made it to the infield and he set the bucket on the pitcher's mound. "You wanna bat first?"

"Sure, but don't—"

"I know. Don't worry. I won't. I'll toss underhand unless you tell me otherwise." He settled my concerns.

"Okay. Thank you." I dug my toe into the dirt and tapped the tip of the metal bat on home plate. Then I lifted the bat and rested it on my shoulders.

"So tennis is still going okay?" Oliver sent the first ball floating my way.

I lifted my left leg and began my step forward as I swung through the ball.

PING!

"Yep," I grunted as I breathed out and followed through. The ball went sailing over Oliver's head into the outfield.

"Nice!" He let go of the next one.

PING!

"Whoa! Look out!" Oliver shouted. The ball was a line drive down the left field line.

"Alright. You can throw overhand and put a little more on it, but nothing crazy." I shimmied my shoulders and bent my knees slightly.

"Do you think we could hit some tennis sometime soon? Or are you too big time now?" Oliver threw the ball with a bit more pace.

WHIFF!

"Well," I chuckled as I missed the ball, "you know how it went the last time we tried. A lot of swinging and not a lot of hitting."

"Sort of like this." He pitched another my way, expecting a miss.

PING!

I sent one almost over the back fence. "Not quite, but I will definitely hit with you again if you really want to. You know I'm always down for more tennis."

"Sweet! Okay. My turn now. Let's switch." He dropped the ball back into the bucket and walked to the plate.

"Here, catch." I tossed the bat up and he grabbed it with one hand.

"You can throw regular to me, okay? I need the practice." Oliver got into his stance.

"Let me get loose. I don't want to send anything too wild your way. I gotta find command of the pitch first." I rolled the ball in my hand before lifting my arms together above my head. Then I took a step backward with my right foot as I began lifting my left leg and rotating my body to the right. My left leg took a deep lunge forward as I effortlessly uncoiled my torso, my throwing arm lagging behind until it naturally zoomed forward like a slingshot.

WHIFF!

"Dang, Tyler! I thought you said you were going to get loose first." Oliver reached his bat out a few times to point it toward the field before bringing it back to rest on his shoulder.

"Sorry. I think all the serving in tennis has made my throwing motion with the ball better without realizing it." I put my palms up and shrugged.

As I sent in more throws, we continued talking.

"Tyler, are you ever going to do anything about Gene? Or are you just going to let your life continue on like it always has been? I don't see how you live with that kind of heaviness on you." He shook his head.

PING!

Then he said, "It's really not healthy, you know, to keep it bottled up like that and to never let it out. You should at least try to say something or talk to him."

Oliver was doing what all good friends did, which was be real with me, but my heart and soul had turned upside down from thirteen years of what felt like mental abuse, even if half of it was self-inflicted from my own mind. Instead of catching and throwing out all the old memories, my head chose to juggle them in a continuous never-ending cycle.

"Things have been fine ever since I stopped talking to him. There's nothing to fix." I hadn't ever told Oliver about the verbal attack at the tennis courts.

PING!

"I don't know about that, Tyler." He wasn't giving in. "Just like you're firing these baseballs my way, you need to send Gene some sort of strong message so he knows. If you don't, you'll carry around this extra weight with you like that bucket full of baseballs."

"Oliver, I have already done that by stepping back and not being around him anymore. That is how I operate, so if that doesn't work, I will have to deal with it. I am honestly okay with how things are right now." I started to grind my teeth ever so slightly, avoiding direct eye contact. "Well, I don't like how I hate being at school, but I am glad I don't have to be around his group of friends anymore." I clenched my jaw and gripped my fingers tightly along the threads. "Can we not talk about it anymore?" I zipped the ball right over the plate.

WHIFF!

"Okay. Okay." Oliver put up his hands in surrender. "Can you take a little off the speed there, mister?"

"Okay. I'm sorry." I threw another one without as much gusto. "You know I get worked up about it. Anyway, I think we can talk about something else now if you want."

"Oh. Actually, I've been meaning to ask you which senior retreat you chose. Please, tell me we picked the same one." Oliver put his palms together with his fingers pointing to the sky.

"Senior retreat?" I scratched my head. School functions weren't my focus area.

"Tyler, the senior retreat." He moved his hands in front of his body with his palms facing upward. "You know how we all have to go to the whole class retreat soon, but then you have to choose a second one to participate in where it's not the entire class?"

"Ohhh…" The light bulb went off in my head. "Yes. I am doing the silent retreat, of course."

"Tyler! Oh my gosh! Why? That one is going to be so boring!

You don't even get to talk!" Oliver shrugged out his frustration. "Tell your advisor to change you to my retreat."

"I'm not doing that because—"

Oliver interjected, "He will be there. I know." He shook his head in disgust. "Tyler, he will always be there, at everything. This is not normal behavior. You are not participating in so many things because of one person. How can you do that? It's not okay." He let out a deep breath and paused for a moment. Then he added, "But I still love ya, bro. At least we will get to be at the all-class retreat together."

"Well, I was going to say that I didn't enjoy sharing my thoughts and feelings to everyone, so the silent retreat seemed like the better option, but thank you for being honest. I am not going to change my selection. It's too late anyhow. Do you care if we leave now?" I stopped throwing and started to walk around the field to put the baseballs back into the bucket. The handle dug into my palm, and as each baseball dropped inside, the imprint pinched deeper. It hurt, but I didn't care. I kept putting one foot in front of the other like I always had.

After leaving the field that day, some of Oliver's words reso-nated in my mind. We went on with our daily school lives, but for me, that meant the negative thoughts returned. I was comparing myself to the other students like I had done at tennis with the rankings. I believed there probably wasn't another kid in the world who was living an amazing life outside of school while also experiencing the worst life ever at it, trying to avoid everyone at all costs. This did not seem normal to me. Maybe Oliver was right, but where could I express these pent-up thoughts?

My senior English teacher ended up being the same lady who

taught my summer course to get into this place. It was funny because back then, she read one of the essays I had written.

"What is this?" She held the paper out to me with red pen marks all over it.

"Ummm . . ."

"I don't see a thesis statement or three key points." She raised her eyebrows and peered over her glasses. "This isn't organized at all. We have some work to do, young man."

"Yes, ma'am." I accepted the paper from her with my head down. "Can you please show me?"

"Of course, Tyler." She spent extra one-on-one time with me that summer until I understood how to properly assemble my introductory paragraph and ultimately grow it into a full essay.

Now it was the first month of senior year, and she was introducing an assignment to us. "Gentlemen, your next essay is an open-ended written task in which you get to select your own topic. I mainly need to see if we can construct a complete essay with strong elaboration in your body paragraphs."

One student raised his hand. "So we can write about anything?"

"Yes," she said, nodding. "If you think it's something you shouldn't write about, then don't. Do we understand?"

In unison, the class responded, "Yes, ma'am."

"Alright. You have the remainder of class to be working on your essay. I will be grading your quizzes from the other day. If you have any questions, please ask." She sat down at her desk and began grading.

Everyone jumped right into working as if they enjoyed it. I guess being allowed to choose what we wanted to write about was a factor. We were so used to being told what to do, but now, we were in the driver's seat directing our own journey.

As I sat there with the cursor blinking on the page in front of me, I hit the button to place it at the top center. My mind searched for interesting topics but couldn't find anything as other things were moving around in my head like Oliver's words: *That is not normal behavior... It's not okay.*

I rested my fingers atop the keyboard and took a deep breath, wondering if I should ask the teacher, but then...

CLICKITY-CLACK-CLACK

The title appeared on the screen one letter at a time.

What Is Normal?

My eyes stared blankly, and my finger rested on the delete button until I slowly pulled it away and back to home row.

My fingers rattled the keyboard and began letting it all out. Once I introduced my main topic and key points, I poured on all the details to further my own thinking about whether I was normal. I mentioned everything most students had in their lives that I had used to create a hole in mine: No football games. No basketball games. No baseball games. No games of any sort. No dances. (Yes, they held dances with the all-girls school.) No parties outside of school. No hanging out. All of this circled back to asking, what is normal? The students who were experiencing all of these didn't seem depressed like me, so there must've been something wrong with how I was choosing to live my life.

BRRRING!

The time had flown by while I was tapping the keys furiously and expressing all the thoughts that had recently been floating around in my head, but some of the weight lifted from my shoulders as I wrote.

"Boys," the teacher said, calling our attention. "I need for you to go ahead and submit what you have before you leave. I will be grading it as a first draft. All of you did a great job focusing today and working hard. Thank you, and I will see you tomorrow."

Without thinking much about it, I clicked save, then submit, and pushed my chair in to head to my next class.

The next day, I sat down when I entered class as usual, but then I noticed my teacher was calling me over using her pointer finger and bright red fingernails. There was a hum of chatter from boys coming into the room.

I made my way to her desk. "Yes, ma'am?"

"Are you doing okay, Tyler?" She put her hand on my shoulder.

"Yeah. I'm fine." The words slipped out of my mouth quickly and I stood up straight to show there couldn't possibly be anything wrong.

"Well, I read your paper." She took her hand back. "You haven't been to a single event your entire time at this school?"

BRRRING!

Before I could respond, she proceeded with starting class. There was genuine concern on her face, but I tried my best to put on a front. She obviously wasn't buying it after feeling every last bit of my heart in that essay. We never finished our conversation at the end of class or the following days. However, I carried a newfound sense of comfort when I walked into her class because she was now aware of my inner battle, and she spoke to me differently moving forward and wasn't as strict.

A higher concern was placed on my mental health. She simply gave me a calm look and an occasional nod, and I sent it back to communicate I was okay. She knew I wasn't, but she continued to show her acknowledgment for what was going on in my world, and that made me feel better.

My other teachers didn't know why I walked around with my hair in my face and my head down. I could tell many of them wondered if I was okay because they tried to say hello to me over the years, but I had grown into a state of not caring while I was at school, and that was the persona I kept. If I could go back, I would apologize to all my teachers because they cared for me, but I couldn't care back.

As the hotter months of the year completely faded away, the cooler temperatures of fall started to take over. The leaves were changing to yellow, red, and a bit of light orange. The football season was well underway. The foliage hovered in the breeze, and with the all-class retreat right around the corner, many of my current and past concerns were doing the same thing in my head. This was going to be the first time in my entire high school life I was going to be around my classmates outside of school. My stomach was already nauseous, and even thinking about it raised my heart rate.

After all, I had spent my entire high school life trying to disappear, and now I would have to be seen and heard, even open up to classmates in deep conversation.

"Everyone, please board the buses!" a teacher belted so all could hear. "Check your retreat packet! It indicates which bus you ride! We are departing in ten minutes!"

Unfortunately, Oliver was on Bus A while I was on Bus B. Over a hundred boys crammed inside the buses, but I never noticed anyone. I boarded mine with my head down and my bangs hanging low so nobody could make eye contact with me, but I could still see my own feet to find a vacant window seat.

"Please listen for your name while we take roll." Another teacher held a clipboard in his hands and reeled off name after name and boys responded appropriately.

"Here!"

"Present!"

"He's not here!"

Gene's name got called, and as I heard his voice for the first time in forever, a piercing chill rippled through my body. I had no idea he was even on the same bus.

Later down the list, it was my turn.

The teacher's voice echoed, "Tyler Richardson!"

I raised my hand silently in an attempt to draw less attention to myself and confirmed through my hair I had been checked off and accounted for.

Once all students were called, the hydraulics of the bus let out a loud hush. The smell of the muffler seeped through the cracks of the windows. We took a slow roll out of the parking lot and made our way onward to our destination at a rural campsite.

The whole ride, I either looked out the window at passing cars or down at my own feet under the seat in front of me. Whoever sat next to me was friends with the boys across the aisle, and they spent their time chatting with each other. Without Oliver to talk to, I was essentially alone.

After about an hour, the same teacher stood and held onto the overhead rack. "Alright, gentlemen. We are here. The agenda is completely full for the entire rest of the day, so we need to follow all directions in order to accomplish all of our goals for today."

The bus rumbled and bumped over a back pebble road as we pulled into the campground. Pine trees surrounded the area. They were as tall as the sky and shielded us from the outside world. A few medium-sized cabins were partially hidden amongst the woods. Dead pine needles blanketed the ground. There were a couple of buildings a bit larger and nicer in quality than the cabins. When we got off the bus, we dropped off our bags and were directed to enter one of these buildings.

We were scheduled to be at the camp for the day and to return to school the following morning.

Ugh. Oh my goodness. Why? How am I going to make it through?

The teachers had us gather around to sing, set the mood, and give thanks for this experience we were about to have together.

"There you are." I found Oliver, hoping I could latch onto him for the day.

"The bus ride was so fun," Oliver whispered. "This is going to be awesommmmmmmme . . ." He faded the end of the word into the hum of the song.

Internally, I shook my head and rolled my eyes. Oliver always tried to throw a positive spin on things, but I wasn't buying in like he and everyone else was.

My insides were numb and had been damaged too much to believe any of this could help me feel better. If I chose to sing, it wouldn't take away the hurt. Following along amongst the sea of normalcy only meant becoming part of the broken system, and I was not about to let that happen.

The singing concluded. "Amen. That was so moving," a teacher proclaimed. "It is absolutely amazing to have the entire senior class together in one place today. I hope you cherish this time together because before you know it, your time at our school will be over, and many of you will move on to bigger and better things. Throughout the last few years, you have grown as a class, but we hope this retreat will make your brotherhood even stronger."

He wiped a tear from under his eye. "I'm sorry. This is emotional for me because this is my tenth year, and I have seen amazing things happen here in the past. But it will be up to you. What you put into this retreat is what you will get out of it. Hanging back, watching, and listening is not the best way to do that. You have to be vulnerable and put yourself out there. I strongly encourage all of you to do this today, and I can't think of a better place to try than in our first activity of small groups. You might not be paired with classmates of your choosing, but that's the point, to get to know everyone a little better. With all of that said, we will now divide you up into groups. When you hear your name, please go with your group's lead teacher, and he or she will direct you from there."

Oh my gosh. I'm going to throw up. Please put me in Oliver's group. Please!

In a matter of seconds, Oliver's name was called.

He looked at me. "You'll be fine, Tyler. It's okay." He hopped off to catch up to his group, and we were separated yet again.

My anxiety meter started to rise, praying I would not be grouped with Gene.

My heart thumped rapidly throughout my body until a small moment of relief came when I realized we would not be together.

Each group walked the campground to find the perfect spot to circle up and huddle in for some serious conversations. My stomach was turning inside out even though I was lucky enough to only have four boys in my group. Some of them were a part of my long-term pain, including Crews, and it was enough to make me collapse into my shell.

We found a spot inside one of the cabins. The teacher instructed us to grab some chairs and make a circle on one side of the room. "Let's go around the circle and say something we are grateful for about our classmates."

When it got to me, I shook my head and mumbled, "I'm not ready." I was invisible at school, and I wanted it to remain that way here too. My type of response was not going to be the cookie-cutter response the other boys were giving. My heart wanted to say how grateful I was for my tennis friends, and if it wasn't for them, I am not sure I could have survived the last few years. My internal battle of not being normal was triggered because nobody else was saying things about others outside our school community. Plus, this was not appropriately responding to the prompt, so I weaseled my way out of truly participating.

Surprisingly, it took a while to circulate around because the other boys, including Crews, were putting in some effort with this task.

The teacher wrapped up round one. "Boys, that was great. I am so proud of your willingness to share and open up. We are going to break for lunch, and then we will meet back here after one hour. You may head to the cafeteria building located on the other side of the grassy knoll."

Tall blades of grass flattened to the ground under my feet as I trekked toward the scent of mysterious campground cafeteria food. Squirrels scampered around the outside of the building and scurried up trees as we got closer. Birds waited atop nearby branches in hope for possible leftovers accidentally dropped by some high school boys. A few classmates who had finished their small group task earlier had obviously already eaten and were sneaking little pieces of bread to their newfound friends.

"Oliver," I called as we both entered from different doorways and got in line.

"Hey." He filed in behind me. "That was great, wasn't it?"

"Ummm . . ." I didn't want to make him feel bad. "It was fine." We each grabbed a tray.

"Oh, come on. Everyone in my group did really well. They stepped up to the plate and really hit it out of the park. Did you participate?" Oliver raised his eyebrows as he leaned over to scoop some sloshy something onto his plate.

"I froze up. You know how I get." I reached over and grabbed an apple.

"Tyler, is that all you're going to eat? Here, take one of these." He grabbed the tongs and placed a turkey sandwich onto my almost empty plate.

"I'm really not hungry. These sorts of activities make my anxiety increase. I'll be lucky enough to make this apple stay down. You know we have to go back and do more of this, don't you?"

"Yes, but remember, it's important to say how you feel and not only sit back and watch everyone else. This is a part of growing up and maturing." Oliver pointed toward one table. "We can sit over here if you want. There's not too many people."

We both simultaneously clanked our trays on top of the table as we pulled out our chairs to sit.

"Tyler, I understand this is hard for you, but this is about getting out of your comfort zone for a tiny little bit."

"Okay, Oliver. It's that my mind makes it a huge bit. I know you're trying to help. If I end up doing anything crazy, you'll be the first to know."

"I have known you for so long now, Tyler, and you always keep to yourself to try and make everyone else happy, but look how much that has taken over your life. Imagine how different things could be." He stuffed his face full of turkey sandwich.

"You have something on your . . ." I pointed to my left cheek and then took one small chomp of my apple.

He wiped off the dollop of mayonnaise with the tip of his finger and licked it.

"You got it." I laughed and took another bite.

"Okay, as your friend, I am challenging you. When we go back to our small groups after lunch, you have to say at least one thing. It won't be that bad."

"Oliver, I can't make any promises. It will all depend on if my mind lets me say anything."

An announcement came over the campground intercom system, which looked like a megaphone at the top of a telephone pole. "Gentlemen, you have ten minutes remaining before you will need to make your way back to your groups."

"What? Already? Were we in line that long?" Oliver scarfed down more of his food.

The clock ticked faster for me because I wanted to prolong returning to the cabin.

"I'm going to go ahead and go, Tyler. I don't want to miss the start of part two. I'll see you later at some point." He grabbed his tray, pushed his chair in, threw away his trash, and skipped through the doorway.

CRUNCH.

I took another slow bite of my apple and savored a few extra minutes of the clock.

Thoughts of how life could be if I changed my approach appeared and disappeared as if there was never a chance they could become real.

Why is this so difficult?

I tossed the apple core into the trash and reluctantly made my way back to my small group.

CREAK.

I swung open the cabin door. Everyone had already made their way back.

"Alright, boys. I hope you had a good lunch. I will go ahead and say this second half of our small group time is a bit lengthy as we will open up even more and get to know each other better. However, this time, it will be completely pressure-free. If you don't want to answer a question, you don't have to, and we will popcorn respond for whoever decides he wants to share each time. How does that sound?" He turned the page on his clipboard to prepare for the next set of questions.

The boys nodded and held their thumbs up.

"Our first question to ponder is about who you look up to and why."

A few seconds went by and one boy jumped right in. "I look up to my mom. She's a single parent. I'm not sure if I have ever mentioned that before, but she doesn't let that hold her back. I want to be exactly like her when I grow up because she has shown me what it means to never quit and to always strive for your dreams no matter what setbacks you have in life."

This particular response caused the other boys to ask further questions about what it had been like to live with only one parent. The conversation went on for at least thirty minutes before we realized nobody else had responded to the question yet. It didn't matter though because the group was showing empathy and concern for this boy's personal life experiences. He was also a popular athlete about to head off to play college football next year, so a part of me wondered if his social status in school was a reason the others were listening intently. This silly little mind game was causing me to second-guess if I should participate.

The time snuck on by while the other boys shared, and by the time they finished discussing the question, it had already been an hour and a half.

"Wow, boys!" The teacher smiled. "That was incredible, and it was only the beginning! Are you guys ready for the next question?"

The group looked at the clock and Crews said, "Man, it feels like we just finished eating five minutes ago."

"Time flies when you're all in on this activity," he agreed. "Well, let's move on to the next question because if it takes us the same amount of time, then we will have to stop after that. Let's see here. During your time in high school, what has been the most positive part for you?"

Oh no. That is the best and worst possible question for me.

I could probably talk for thirty minutes about this if I answered it in full truth, but I knew I had to alter my answer. My pointer finger slowly raised in the air.

"Yes, Tyler. Go ahead." The teacher pointed to me.

Oliver's voice kept whispering in my head to say something, and I wanted to make him proud even though my face was already turning red.

"Tennis has really been a positive thing for me in high school. I have enjoyed being able to be on the tennis team here and to try and represent the school as best as I can." Then I stopped talking, but everyone was waiting for me to say more. The crickets were coming out early even though it wasn't yet nighttime. The sweat started to trickle inside my shirt.

Instead of the boys asking me any related questions, they didn't say anything to me. One seemed to lean over to another to indicate he didn't even know I was on the tennis team.

"I'm sorry. I forgot the rest of what I was going to say." I broke the awkward silence with my little lie.

The teacher remained encouraging. "That's okay, Tyler. I am so glad you shared. Let's move on to whoever wants to go next."

Oliver, I hope you're happy. That was awful!

Almost two more hours went by, and all I could think about was my tennis family, and how I wanted to say how much they had impacted my life during high school. Since I didn't want to make my classmates feel bad, I never added to my first portion because the truth hurts sometimes. For me, that meant explaining how those within this school community didn't care about or accept me as much as Peyton, Easton, Campbell, and the whole tennis gang.

Eventually, our allotted time came to a close.

Thank goodness that was now finished so we could have our break and get to the final event, which meant one more item off the checklist before I could go back home. I chose to take a solo walk around the camp during our downtime. There was a small pond, so I went over to it to skip some rocks. Part of me felt like the rock in the sense that I was barely touching the surface of my issues, skirting along in life because my mind believed I would be swallowed whole at some point. When I ran out of the thin, disk-like rocks, I began launching some of the more baseball-sized ones high into the air. They hovered in the sky for a half second before gravity grabbed them and pulled them down to the water.

SPLASH!

The heavy weight came crashing down, breaking the plane of the surface as water splashed into the air, and circles of never-ending ripples continued to grow all the way to the edge of the pond. I hurled a few more to see the power each one carried and how it seemed to have an effect on the entire surface area. I reflected and wished I had that kind of strength within me so others would take notice of my pain.

The scratch of the intercom turned on. "Gentlemen, it is now time for dinner. You know where to go. We only have thirty minutes for dinner before we have our next activity. So let's eat quickly and get ready. Thank you."

This time I was unable to find Oliver until I noticed he had already gotten his food and was eating with some other classmates. The dinner options were a repeat of lunch, but my stomach was growling, so I grabbed two turkey sandwiches this time because I had no idea what was coming with our next event. I figured I had made it through the most difficult part of the retreat.

Since we had such a short amount of time, I sat by myself and wolfed down the two sandwiches. As I was taking a sip of water, the loudspeaker came on again. "Boys, it is that time. Everyone needs to make their way to the other building that is catty-corner from where we first started our day today. We will see you there shortly."

Everyone threw away their stuff, and a sea of over a hundred boys began marching to the nearby building. The sun was setting. Real crickets were chirping this time. The birds were flying low to snatch some nighttime bugs. A few squirrels snagged some left-over morsels that had made their way outside the cafeteria doors. My body was a bit more relaxed because I had eaten. I walked in a manner as if we were almost finished and about ready to go to bed soon. There was nothing to worry about anymore.

We poured into the open room. Many boys were reuniting with their friends after having been split up during the break-out sessions.

A teacher grabbed the microphone on the stage and announced, "Alright, boys. Find a spot on the floor. We will be right back to give the instructions." He left the stage.

"Hey, let's go sit over here," reverberated around the room, yet it was never directed toward me. I surveyed the tightly filled area and plopped down on the hard carpet with enough space to spread my legs out in front of me and stretch my arms backward with my palms on the ground.

We were in a large, carpeted room about the size of a basketball court with no chairs anywhere. They told us to get comfortable because we would be here for a while. We all sat and faced the stage that was at the far front of the long room. The stage had two sets of steps, one on the far left and one on the far right, with a microphone standing tall at center stage. The lights began to dim in the entire room except for the bright lights that lit up the stage. I was seated midway back, left side. Gene and his followers were about the same distance back but on the far right and a little bit up.

All the teachers and adults who had come on the retreat were in the room, and one teacher went up to the microphone to explain the rules for Open Mic. It was actually the teacher who had addressed Gene and Kevin that one day in freshman social studies.

"Okay. So I know many of you have heard about Open Mic from previous years' students, and now you are going to find out what that is and have the opportunity to experience it."

I sat there thinking I was glad tomorrow we were going back home, even though it was only one day, and I would be reunited with my tennis friends.

The teacher continued, "So here are the rules for Open Mic. It is now eight p.m. For three total hours, all the adults and teachers are going to leave this room. There will not be anybody in here except for all of you senior boys. During this time, anyone can come onto the stage behind this microphone and say anything he wants to the senior class. Anything. You don't have to worry about us hearing because none of the teachers will be in here. At eleven p.m., we will come back, and Open Mic will be finished. Are there any questions?"

Dead silence.

Wow. Three hours is a long time.

The teacher concluded by stating, "Okay. Once we all leave the room, you may begin." He left the stage. After about thirty seconds, all the teachers had exited. The door slowly closed, and you could hear the *click* as it shut.

CHAPTER 16

Everybody sat there without muttering a sound. *Who in the world is going to go up there first?!* I was definitely never going to do that. An entire two minutes passed without anyone flinching. I honestly had a hunch that as soon as one person started to whisper, it would slowly turn into talking, and then everyone would have a chill session for three hours chitchatting with their friends where they were sitting. I didn't foresee this activity being productive in any way, shape, or form.

Suddenly, one boy got up and walked to the far-right steps of the stage and made his way over to the microphone. I could already hear Gene and company snickering. This particular boy was an easy target, so they were probably sitting over there saying, "What an idiot." Either way, the boy stood tall and began to address the hundred-something souls in the room.

"I want to say I love you guys, and this is the best senior class ever. I also want to say thank you to my best friends—" He listed their names individually. "You guys will always be a part of my life. Thank you for the memories." He bumped his fist on his chest, held it out, and walked off the stage, and before he could completely exit, another boy stood up and he began his trek to the stage and stood behind the microphone.

"What's up, senior class? I want to say y'all are my family. I couldn't have made it through without y'all. I really struggled with the academics of this school, but y'all really helped me out and helped me succeed." He led another shout-out of recognition to some close friends before finishing. "Aight, senior class. Love you guys." With his fist balled up like the other boy, he kissed part of his hand and held up the peace sign as he left the stage.

A good mood had been set with this boy because he had mentioned something vulnerable about himself regarding his academics. It only took one person to open up like that, which touched people's hearts, and it caused more and more boys to go up to the stage and not hold back. The other reason it worked was because this boy was a very popular basketball star for our school. If somebody from the unpopular crowd had started this trend, and if we had heard chuckles in the crowd, then nobody else would have wanted to go up on stage. But because he had many popular friends, nobody laughed, and that set the stage for the rest of the night.

After a while, nobody waited for the person to be finished before they approached the far-right steps of the stage. Each person wanted to make sure he got his chance to say something.

The mood became more serious as different students began to approach the stage and open up even more.

"Hey, senior class. I need to say thank you to [friend one] and [friend two]. Back when we were freshman, I was having a really hard time in my life, and I attempted suicide, but I was unsuccessful. If it wasn't for the two of you, I don't think I would be here today. You guys are the reason I kept going, and I don't know how else to thank you. I love you guys. Stay strong." He nodded and went back to his spot on the floor.

Wow. That was intense. Suicide? I mean, that's serious.

Now all ears were open. There were even more boys that had gone up to say the same thing about suicide, but even during some of those moments on stage, I still heard Gene and his friends snickering. My mind created the dialogue of how they were making fun of each person. "Ha. You should've killed yourself."

I didn't trust I had a good reason to go on stage, but hearing them across the room even though I could barely see them in the darkness, I knew there was no way I would ever go up to that microphone.

More boys waited in line on the side of the stage as one by one another boy approached the microphone.

"Guys. It has been a great four years, and I don't want it to be over. After we all graduate, I don't think we should forget about each other once we go off to college, get married, and have kids. If I ever see any of you ten years from now or further down the road, I want it to be like time never passed. We shouldn't ignore one another if we pass each other in the future. Love y'all."

Things took a sharp left turn when one boy got behind the microphone. "*@#% you! *@#% all of you!" He was breathing heavily. "I'm sorry. That's how I feel. None a y'all care about me. Ever since I came to this school, just because I am Latino, you ignored me and the others like me. Treated us less. You coulda learned about us and our culture, but instead, you chose to put us on an island and leave us there to suffer. This school is messed up, man." He shook his head and confidently returned to be near those he trusted.

How in the world did a fight not break out?

But when he did that, there was a sense of guilt among the room because after all of the small groups and team-building activities of the day, many of the boys had grown closer, and people felt bad he had to go up there and say those things. It seemed to be our fault for not reaching out when we had the chance.

This boy's mini-speech had my mind and emotions spinning as I constantly looked at the stage, but I always took a moment after every person to look over in Gene's direction to see his reaction amongst his friends. I began thinking really hard. That boy who had just gone up there had a lot of courage. I envisioned standing on the stage, looking out at the sea of faces, clearing my throat, and shocking everyone with everything I needed to say.

Why couldn't I have that kind of bravery? Why couldn't I go up on that stage and address Gene and his friends? Why couldn't I go up there and say how difficult they had made everything for me over the years?

Maybe I should, but I never will. But I really want to. But I won't. Gosh, just do it. No. You can't . . .

I heard the voices inside my head fighting.

My classmates continued, and even more followed suit after that one boy and expressed their frustrations toward the senior class or to certain people. This just made me even more depressed as I sat there battling my emotions about going on stage. It would never happen. Not in a million years.

But all these other boys have done it! Ugh!

The good vibes spread around the room, and the time was flying. We hadn't realized how intently we had been listening to all the speakers.

Another boy got up there and began to say, "Back when we were freshman, I used to be friends with [friend's name], but after we had a major argument halfway through the year, we weren't friends anymore. I want to say the argument was all my fault, and I am sorry for even making it happen. I hope you can forgive me because I am truly sorry." He put his hands together in the praying position, shook them lightly, and then left with his head down.

The patterns began to emerge as many boys said very similar things as others. Many mentioned suicide. Many apologized for an old tiff. Some thanked their best friend. There were a few that yelled at everyone. However, the only thing on my mind was wanting to go up on stage, but knowing I would never physically do it. So many boys had gone up there, and it felt like almost everyone had been except for me.

All of a sudden, "Allllrighhht, everyone! It's eleven o'clock!"

Out the windows, it was pitch black. I hadn't even noticed the sun had fully set a long time ago.

"Nooooooooooooooooooooo . . ." echoed from the crowd of boys spread out across the carpeted floor.

"It's eleven p.m. We told you three hours. It has been three hours. It's late, and we have to get up early in the morning." He gave a smile with his mouth closed as if he was thinking.

"Nooooooooooooooo... pleaaaaaaaaasssseee? Can we have just a little bit longer?"

He took a moment and looked at the teachers who were standing in the doorway. They all shrugged and raised their eyebrows as if they didn't mind. So he turned back toward us. "Okay, we'll give you one more hour." That hour flew by so fast as the good vibes in the room continued, and before we knew it, he was back on the stage.

"Allllllrrriiiight, boys! It's midnight!"

"Nooooooooooooooo! Pleeeeeeaaaaaasssssseee?"

"Gentlemen. Listen. It is midnight. We have breakfast at seven a.m. followed by our senior retreat group photo. Then we are immediately getting on the bus and going home. It is too late. We can't let you stay up past midnight." He stood firm with his hands on his hips.

I could hear continued complaints up at the front of the room where boys were addressing the teacher and saying things to him. It was more pleas for extra time. You wouldn't think we needed more after four solid hours of this, but for some reason, we wanted it. It seemed to give me more time to try and convince myself to go on stage and have this weight lifted off my shoulders, but the consequences of saying something were way too risky.

This time, the teacher went to talk to the group of teachers. After they were huddled up for about a minute, he addressed the senior class again. "Okay. We can make a deal with you. We can all go to bed right now, and if you all truly want more time, we can let you wake up early and come back in here from six to seven. After that, we eat breakfast, take the group photo, then leave."

A somewhat unified, "Okay! Yes!"

We all left the room and headed for our cabins to go to bed. I lay there with my eyes open, looking at the ceiling. I don't think I ever fell asleep because all I could do was sit there and think, "I have one more chance to do this if I want to, and if I don't, life will continue to always be the same." I imagined myself as the heavy rock doing a cannonball into the pond, but the pond was the stage, and my words were the rock. The impact might reach further than I could ever hope. But then I realized how heavy my words could be, and if they hit too hard, they could hurt, yet my intentions were to fix the pain.

If I slept at all, it was only for a couple hours.

Before I knew it, they woke us up with just enough time for our sleepy heads to waddle back over to that large, carpeted room with our eyes half closed. My mind had shifted to wondering if this morning would be as good as last night. I kept thinking it seemed as if almost everyone who was willing to go up there had, and was anyone even going to approach the stage after all the begging to continue last night. Would it even be as powerful? Would the positive vibes fill the room again?

It was officially six a.m. We were all seated on the floor. The same teacher went behind the microphone with coffee in hand. "Good morning, gentlemen. As you requested, this will be your final hour of Open Mic. There will not be any extra time, so if you haven't come up here yet, and you have been wanting to, then this is your last chance. At seven, this exercise is officially complete, and we will then have to go to the cafeteria area for breakfast followed by our group photo at eight. We will then load up the buses and head home. You may begin once we leave the room." He left the stage, and the adults exited the room.

CLICK!

We sat there rubbing our eyes to try and wake up while we waited for the first boy to approach the microphone.

Without any hesitation, one boy went up there, and it was obvious he had been waiting all night thinking about this and didn't want to waste a single moment before it was too late. He first addressed a few of his friends in a positive manner, but then he, like many others, mentioned having attempted committing suicide. Tears rolled down his face. He thanked his friends for being there for him. They all waited for him at the bottom of the steps and gave him a group hug.

The mood had been set. Everyone was awake now for sure, and all eyes and ears were on the stage as more and more boys formed a short waiting line of about four to five on the side of the steps until each boy finished.

This hour was flying by, and my opportunity was slipping away. It felt a little different this morning because the sunlight was peeking through the windows, so there was no hiding from anyone. I could clearly see Gene, who probably couldn't believe we had to get up for another hour of this. As more boys spoke, the time ticked away. A half an hour had already passed. Then forty minutes. Fifty.

My heart was racing.

The line on the side of the stage appeared like this: a couple dozen boys standing atop the stage, right above the steps. Then about three boys sitting on the side steps, and maybe twelve boys standing at the bottom of the steps.

Approximately five footsteps away from the stage steps were some double doors, which were the exit doors to go outside. There were other entryways and exits into this room, but these particular double doors were the closest to the cafeteria on the campground. We had over a hundred seventeen- and eighteen-year-old boys who hadn't eaten breakfast and had been awake now for an hour. Many of them were getting antsy about wanting food.

When it was about eight minutes or so until the top of the hour, slowly but surely, a small crowd began to form near those double doors. I found it very disrespectful to do that while other boys were still pouring their hearts out on stage. I wondered why people couldn't wait another five minutes to line up.

As I had been doing between speakers, I looked over to where Gene had been sitting to see his reaction yet again, but he wasn't there. I scanned the room and quickly discovered him amongst the small crowd by the double doors. *He doesn't care what these people have to say.*

I looked back to the stage to intently listen to the person speaking, but now that Gene was in a much clearer view to me, it was hard not to look back where he was after every minute or so. The next time I glanced over, he was doing something many boys did, which was pushing and shoving people out of the way.

Are you serious? Is breakfast that important you must get in front of the other twelve boys who are standing over at the doors? Why can't you be thirteenth in line?

Yet again, I was more frustrated for the speaker who wasn't being listened to by a good majority of the audience now. I made sure I was at least one of the good listeners as I looked back at the boy who was currently speaking.

The next time I looked over, I couldn't really see where Gene was, but I assumed he had made his way to first in line by the doors and had been swallowed by the now swarm of boys near the exit. As my eyes began to move back toward the stage, they did a double take because I thought I saw him. Yes, for some reason, he had moved closer to the steps of the stage.

It was 6:55 a.m., and when I looked back again, he was standing on the first step leading up to the stage. Then, a little bit higher on the steps a moment later. I swore he was looking for somebody to let a friend know it was time for breakfast, and he needed to claim his position in line before he couldn't anymore. I scanned all the boys up there, and I began guessing who he was trying to find and surely convincing myself who it was, but Gene didn't seem to be shoving people anymore.

All of a sudden, in slow motion in my mind, he walked to the microphone.

Oh... my... gosh... What in the world could he possibly say?

It almost felt like he had beaten me up there like how he had always beaten me in life, and now I really lost my opportunity to speak up. I thought he was going to grab the microphone and say, "Hey guys, it's time for breakfast! Let's go!" and walk off the stage. Instead, this is what actually transpired . . .

With his head hanging low, but his eyes looking into the crowd, he leaned into the mic. "First, I probably need to apologize to every single person in this room... "

People sat up straight and started to whisper but quickly stopped to hear the rest.

My jaw was on the floor, and my eyes were wide open. Goosebumps covered my entire body, and a small pond started to form between my eyelids as I couldn't believe what I was hearing.

"...because I have probably made fun of every single person here, so I am sorry for that." He had a crackle of nerves in his voice and stepped back for a moment. The sun was now shining right where he was standing.

Wow. I don't know what to say right now. How did that just happen? And for him to realize it on his own? I mean, do you honestly think somebody addressed him and said, "Hey, Gene. I think you should go up there and apologize to everyone because you have said something bad about all of them?" No! Nobody did that! Somehow, some way, he thought of going up there on his own!

He surprisingly continued and leaned back into the microphone.

"Now, I really need to apologize to a specific person." He waited a few seconds before saying, "Henry Wilson. We used to be really good friends when we were freshmen and sophomores, but then we let a girl get between our friendship, and I am really sorry for that."

He stepped back again and put his hands in his pockets.

Okay. That was nice. He's trying to make amends with that boy. I haven't seen him attempt that before.

Gene swayed and slightly turned as if about to exit stage left. However, he had one last thing to say. At this moment, the world stopped. I didn't see the crowd of boys at the double doors. I didn't see the sunlight coming in the windows anymore. I had been thinking how in the world was Gene up on this stage right now, and how was he seemingly being a good person? After all these years, it now took a small turn with Gene addressing his apology to the entire senior class.

He took his hands out of his pockets and grabbed the microphone.

"But most of all, I need to apologize to Tyler Richardson for making his life a living hell. I'm sorry."

He placed the mic back on the stand and walked off the stage with his head down.

The pond that had formed on my eye had been hit by Gene's

words, and a small tear rolled down my cheek. I quickly wiped it off so nobody would see.

My ears were ringing, my head was spinning. I was in complete shock. I didn't know what to do next. Everything was still in slow motion. I couldn't discern anything anybody was saying. The only thing I could hear were those words already replaying inside my head, *But most of all… But most of all.* Thirteen years of mental abuse boiled down to thirty seconds of my senior year.

I don't even remember if anyone spoke after him. Oliver, who I hadn't noticed was sitting a few rows of people in front of me, immediately turned around with his mouth wide open and smiled at me. I was in utter shock and bewilderment, but I felt good in a strange way I couldn't verbalize yet. I never could have expected this curveball moment to fall into place when and where it did. It didn't seem real at first. A couple other students who didn't even really know me leaned over to where I was sitting to say they never even realized Gene and I knew each other.

What seemed like only a minute after Gene dropped his bombshell onto the stage, the teacher waltzed right up there and declared Open Mic officially over. I was still dazed and confused. *Who cares about breakfast anymore? I just experienced one of the biggest moments of my life.* However, the teacher continued and reminded everybody we were now having breakfast followed by our group photo. I had to immediately snap out of it, stand up, and head over to the door, exiting my emotions and leaving behind what was probably the most meaningful thing I had heard in at least a decade of school.

I let the crowd rush out the door as I slowly started my walk to the cafeteria, simultaneously trying to find Gene.

Oliver found me again while walking over and asked, "Can you believe that? Did you talk to him yet?" He put his arm around my shoulder.

"I can't believe it either. I haven't had a chance to find him yet." I looked over my shoulder.

Then, in the blink of an eye, there he was: Gene. I immediately addressed him as we continued to walk toward the cafeteria. I didn't care who was around. It was like I was still shut off from the rest of the world.

"First, I cannot believe you even went up there, Gene, so thank you for simply going up there to do what you did because I know that wasn't easy. Thank you for apologizing to everybody and to me. It really means a lot to me. I'm speechless. I can't even explain. Thank you."

He replied, "I really mean it, man. I'm sorry. I know I haven't made things easy for you over the years." And we sort of bro-style hugged it out as we walked to the cafeteria. If you had asked me who I was most likely to hug at this retreat, my answer would have never been Gene—not in a million years. Yet, here we were, defying logic.

We grabbed our breakfast and sat at the same table. Only the two of us. It was another surreal moment. How was I sitting there with Gene, somehow feeling on top of the world, when I had spent the last thirteen years trying to figure out how to get him out of my life? I don't remember any of our conversation at the table.

Before I knew it, it was time for our senior class photo. There I was with my long hair and all I'd been hiding behind for so many years in high school, standing directly next to Gene, smiling.

SNAP!

That picture is my only physical memory from that day. I don't even remember the date. All I know was that moment changed my life forever.

CHAPTER 17

I was dubious about what had transpired at the retreat. Had it been a dream, a mirage of sorts? I still couldn't believe it had actually happened. Not only that, but years of negative reinforcement taught me to be guarded and protective of my feelings. I felt trapped. Did that little positive moment in time trump the thousands of bad days I endured throughout my childhood? Did thirty seconds mean Gene was a changed person? Would I be put in his crosshairs again and entrapped? What about all the other boys who followed in Gene's ways? Jackson, Crews, Kevin. What if Gene changed, but they didn't? I had more questions than answers—all of them based on fear, the deadliest emotion on earth. Fear has broken up marriages, destroyed countries, and started world wars. How could I escape the clutches of this unbreakable bond?

Fairly quickly after the retreat, I recalled things changing, but there was a hesitancy to see if it would last. Not only was Gene being nice to me, but so were the other boys who had put some of that added pressure on me over the years.

"Hey, Tyler. Do you want to sit with us at lunch today?" Gene asked.

"Sure." I accepted the invitation with a lump in my throat. The welcoming nature shocked me. It had been so long since I had sat with this group of people, and my only memories of these types of school meals together did not have positive connotations connected with them.

When the time came, I joined their table, and even Crews pulled out a chair for me. "Tyler, here you go. Have a seat."

I set my lunch down and prepared to watch their behavior and conversations closely.

Then Jackson asked, "So, Tyler, what's the update on tennis? I heard you won a national tournament. Is that true?"

"Yes, but it was just doubles."

"Seriously?" Gene raised his eyebrows. "That's insane. Like a real national tournament? You got first place?"

Crews added, "In the United States?"

"Yes," I muttered softly. I was never one to try and one-up these guys.

"That is so cool." Gene was making me feel like my life was starting to matter.

"Do you think you might play in college?" Jackson asked.

"Well, actually, yes. I have been offered a scholarship." I still mumbled a bit because I didn't like to boast.

"Oh, wow. Do you know if it's division two, three?" Crews asked.

"It's division one."

"Dang." Crews looked at the others, and they all opened their mouths in awe.

"So are you guys doing basketball or football in college?" I genuinely believed this was in their future because they were the ones who had spent their whole lives being so competitive in baseball, basketball, and football.

"Nah," each of them moaned.

"We wish though," Gene said.

Somehow, I was the only one who was going to move on to play college athletics.

For a moment it felt good, but then I wished they had this same opportunity to play a sport in college too.

As we ate our lunch, I observed their words with each other carefully, but nothing struck a chord of déjà vu from the past. They weren't just being kind. That is not what did it for me. It was how I wasn't hearing those unnecessary, opinion-filled comments about other people. It was like they had suddenly matured, at least during school hours.

The real test was when Gene asked me to do something I had not done my entire high school life. "Tyler, you wanna go to the football game with us Friday night?"

My curiosity to see if they could keep this up helped me accept yet another invitation.

I remember showing up, and Gene even waved me over and introduced me to a friend of his. "Hey, Tyler. What's up? This is great, isn't it?" There were people everywhere cheering on our football team.

I simply enjoyed the moment, but I was also on guard wondering when it would go back to normal. The real Gene. Because this was still unreal.

That evening, lying in bed, I realized I survived my first school social outing, and I had actually enjoyed it.

Is this a dream? Am I going to wake up and realize this never happened?

In class the following week, I couldn't remember if I had written about it in a paper or if the English teacher overheard us talking about the football game, but somehow, she found out I had attended. She tilted her head and squinted her eyebrows. "So, you went to a game?" She was so confused and shocked after having recently read my emotion-filled paper, 'What Is Normal?' Yet she was elated and gave me a soft pat on the back, smiling from ear to ear. She knew how big of a deal this was for me.

The year continued, but that one football game was the final one of the season. Then basketball began. There was a game every Friday night, and after the game, Gene and his friends always ate out at the same restaurant. I went to the first basketball game, sat with Gene, and also joined them for dinner. Nobody talked negatively about anyone whether they were present or not.

"That was a great game," Gene told the group.

"Yeah," Jackson agreed. "I feel bad for Micah though. He barely missed the last shot to win the game."

"Speaking of… here he is! Our champion!" Gene welcomed Micah as he entered the doors of the restaurant. "Good game, man. Don't worry about the ending. If you weren't on the team, we never would even have a chance in half of our games. You'll get the next one."

Crews gave Micah a fist bump.

"That one boy on the other team was lights out from beyond the arc," Jackson said. "There was no stopping him. I wish he played for our school."

The positivity flowed our entire time together. This helped ease many of the words that used to hover around in my head. I was beginning to build new audio and visual recordings to hold onto in my memory bank.

I decided to go to the next basketball game and dinner. Then to the next one. And the next. I went to all the games. Gene was there at all of them.

He had changed. They had changed. It was becoming real.

I continued making up for my lost time in high school, and I went to the homecoming dance and brought a date I had met through tennis. We went with Gene's group. Later in the year, we did the same thing for prom. When baseball season came, I went to all those games too.

As I had grown older, I developed a strong artistic talent in drawing and painting, and I discovered I could express myself in another way besides writing down my thoughts. When I became a senior, I had signed up for the advanced art class.

My final piece in the senior art show at the end of the year was a representation of my entire high school life, including my senior year. It consisted of numerous images all hand-drawn with pencil on poster-sized white paper. The first was of The Scream painting by Edvard Munch with the man on the bridge in sheer terror, depicting my fear of following Gene into the unknown. The bridge led over to the prestigious Taj Mahal, giving the false notion everything would be wonderful in this place. Right behind that was the swirling fright of Vincent van Gogh's *Starry Night* suddenly surrounding me with a heavy gloom.

To the right of these illustrations, there was an elongated metal wristwatch extending from the top of the paper to the bottom, completely trapping me in the shadow of Gene for so many years. Next was the chilling profile of Marilyn Manson, illustrating this depressing time in my life and all the frustration deep within me. The watch and Manson together symbolized how I was so angry for a very long time, and because of that, the next image was the *Mona Lisa*. The painting by the Italian Renaissance artist Leonardo da Vinci was famous because throughout history those who viewed this masterpiece couldn't decide if she was smiling or not. I, like the *Mona Lisa*, had tried to keep a straight face on the outside where people might have thought I was okay, but on the inside, I was not.

Next in line was a baseball pitcher who had just released a

baseball flying in the viewer's direction. The ball was larger than life as it came closer to the plate and further away from the pitcher. There were distinct airfoil lines drawn to show the ball was carving a crazy path through the air like a curveball. This was the moment Gene launched the biggest curveball of my life that I wasn't prepared for, and it definitely hit me hard, but in the most unpredictable and positive way.

Lastly, the fourth and final image for my senior art project was of a muscular matador taking a bull by the horns.

The determined man was in danger of being pushed off a cliff by the raging bull. However, the man held his ground and methodically pushed back to overcome the beast. The drawing exemplified how I pushed away from the thoughts that had always haunted me, taking the metaphorical bull by the horns to move on from adversity and negativity to become happy, healthy, and successful.

My senior project was a visual study in perseverance. But my primary education was littered with obstacles and revelations about life, love, and the pursuit of happiness.

Senior year ended. We graduated, and I moved away for college. We never saw each other ever again, but this whirlwind journey had shaped my future before I knew it.

CHAPTER 18

I played four great years of college tennis, but I noticed a disturbing pattern emerge with my teammates. In doubles, you have a partner, and whenever I had to be the dominant partner leading our duo to victory, it didn't go well. On the other hand, if my partner verbally directed our strategy during the match, like Jimmy had done for me, we tended to have greater success. I realized, because of my past, I was a better sidekick than a leader on the court. I was really in tune with my partner's wants and needs and could produce the required output as needed. This had made a winning strategy on and off the court, and we had a winning record my senior year.

After college, I became a teacher within the secondary school system. How about that? I guess it was destiny since I consider the worst years of my life to have occurred during that time. It's as if I am now here to look out for adolescents who are suffering like I had. My professional experience has been in the public school system, and as you can imagine, a lot of verbal bullying occurs. Many students act like the adult doesn't even exist, and they can say some of the harshest things. When a student asks for help, sometimes it is hard for me to know exactly how to help them since I wasn't even able to help myself when I experienced it.

The incidents get documented if they're serious, but it's the sly, under-the-radar comments made by kids over time that are not easy to detect, and they know how to beat the system. If a kid goes crying to the counselor about being bullied, it tends to get looked at as a one-time offense when really, we all know it has probably been much more than that. Or they don't go crying to anyone because they are too afraid of the repercussions.

In addition to my primary occupation, being a tennis teaching professional has been an additional source of income. How ironic is that, since the way I started tennis was because of a trick by Gene and company? I should probably thank him for that.

How was it that Gene changed my life? It was his simple apology. As soon as he did that and backed it up by showing his new ways, it helped erase all of the judgmental and negative behaviors that constantly juggled around in my head. Since he was able to do that for me, I ended up thinking about my friend, Easton, the one who had the girlfriend and tried to plead for forgiveness from me about our broken friendship. I had not granted it to him. Twelve years had passed, and during one spring break trip back to my hometown, I discovered Easton still lived there, and I hadn't spoken with him in all those years. I never even knew where he had gone to college, or how far he went with his tennis.

I had been hanging out with old friends for an entire week, and I had only one more full day before I would have to return to my current home city. There was not a lot of time if I wanted to attempt to contact Easton, to try and see him in person.

On the night before my last day, I picked up my phone around nine forty-five, and I dialed a number I found online for a new athletic store he had started.

RING-RING... RING-RING...

Suddenly, it switched over to an automated Google voice system. "Please press one for store hours and information, or press two to continue."

I took a deep breath and pressed the number two.

The robot voice continued, "Please state your name after the beep."

BEEP!

"Tyler Richardson," I said loud and clear.

RING-RING... RING-RING... RING-RING... RING-RING ...

I figured it was pretty late at night, and this was apparently the phone number to his business, so I didn't think anybody would answer. I was completely prepared for leaving a voicemail when...

"Hello, this is Easton."

Oh my gosh! It's him!

I jumped right in before I could decide to retreat. "Hi, Easton. This might come as a big shock or surprise to you, but this is Tyler Richardson, and I am calling because I am in town, and I know way back in the day I didn't do a good job of accepting your apology, so I am calling you to say I am sorry, and I didn't know if you would want to meet up before I left town to try and catch up a little."

Without hesitation, Easton responded, "Wow. Hey, don't worry about it, man. It's all good. I would love to meet up." He had a smile in his voice.

And so we did, and it wasn't until we met later the next day that I found out Easton had really been struggling with some things in his life, and he was going through a twelve-step addiction program. He had just left class right before I had called him. Out of those twelve steps, the one he was now assigned to complete was this: address a past conflict in your life with somebody. Wow. Can you believe that? Amazing.

Those thirteen years of torture around Gene were awful while they were happening, and luckily, I was able to outlast it. However, honestly, I wouldn't change any of it because it made me into the person I am today, one who encourages and lifts others up no matter who they may be. After that experience, I further developed my self-awareness regarding how to speak to others so that all people feel important and included.

Despite my inability to see it during those difficult years, I am beyond thankful for receiving the support I did from my family. Having my sister there to stand up for me and to listen when I needed to vent about Gene meant the world to me. Not only that, but she was a living example of how to be strong and not care what others thought.

My parents were likely confused about some of my behaviors growing up, but it was my fault for not opening up to them. They did the best they knew how to do and provided so much love and care for me even though I wasn't clearly communicating about my issues. My dad spent so much time with me developing my hand-eye coordination and athletic skills. My mom worked so hard to make sure I received a very high level of education and top-quality tennis training. At the time, I was blind to the love they were giving me, but now, as an adult, it is obvious to me all of the blessings they were bestowing upon me.

I still try my best to live by those same words I ranted off onto paper in the school library that year, when the English teacher couldn't comprehend my debate about never being able to fully know why an artist created something if we haven't asked him or her. This paper expressed how strongly I wanted to make sure I never acted like Gene for the rest of my life. The effects from the long-term trauma still linger today. Every now and then, somebody will say something that triggers a past memory of how Gene would say things, and it sends me back in time to my childhood. I am not sure how long this will last, but I know I need to keep pushing forward in life.

After a few years of being a school teacher, I decided to do something long overdue—the talent show. Remember, I had dropped out of my school's talent show at the last minute, fearing retribution by Gene and friends. I never got to perform my much-practiced juggling routine. Even though this was many years later into my adulthood, I was still very nervous to step onto the stage. I knew the audience might share negative opinions about my performance, but this was something that had to be done.

I planned to perform the same Master Juggler Test series I learned as a third grader. It had been twenty years since I had dropped out of the talent show. I felt since Gene had gotten up on stage for me when he might have been nervous, then I could muster up the courage to do the same. But I added an element to my show that wouldn't have been there all those years ago. I needed to take a stand for all the other kids out there like me, so I had my own idea for how to be the rock that would catapult into the pond and ripple outward to affect all the audience members as well as the participants.

I performed my juggling act while words scrolled across a dropdown screen next to me about what it's like to juggle bullies, and the overall message was to not be a bully. I was the opening act, sort of an icebreaker, so the following acts could feel more comfortable about being on stage.

I would like to conclude with my performance from the talent show after becoming a teacher, and my greatest hope is this will be the opening act that sparks a change in many people's futures.

The entire student body had entered the auditorium and everyone was jammed shoulder-to-shoulder in the audience. The hum of conversations reverberated off the walls until someone hit the lights. The room was dark except for the spotlight on the stage. To lead off the show, a teacher stepped onto the far left of the stage in front of a closed, red curtain and grabbed the microphone.

"When you watch this act, please listen carefully to the words, and also watch the words as they go across the screen. This act is not just to show a specific talent but to also show the effects of bullying, and how bullying can occur with someone at a young age and impact them for a long time even after the bullying has stopped. It is my pleasure to introduce a very special friend and talented teacher… "

The screen lowered, the curtains opened, and the bright lights filled the stage as the music began. The words from my self-recorded audio started to tell a story that shared the bitter truth but was filled with inspiration and triumph to overcome some of life's greatest fears.

JUGGLING BULLIES

Life is already hard enough to juggle
There's lots of ups and downs
It's even harder when you juggle things in your mind

Was just a third grader
Who knew how to juggle
Signed up for the talent show

Practiced forever
A long time
For nothing

Comments of bullies juggled in my mind
What if somebody says this about me
What if they say that about me

I can juggle
I can't juggle bullies

I can't juggle the comments
I can't juggle the laughs
I can't stand up to them

All I can do is juggle
But not anymore
Not in the third-grade talent show
I can't do it

Twenty years later
Here I am
The same thoughts in my head

Terrified of the comments
Terrified of the laughs
But I hope they have changed

My first talent show ever
Since chickening out in third grade
And watching from the crowd
The easy place to be

Juggling is hard
Especially when you juggle bullies
In your mind

So help these students today
To not have to juggle bullies
Don't be a bully

AUTHOR'S NOTE

This book was something that came about after I became a teacher. Many students came to me over the years to express troubling times they were experiencing. I found myself always telling them this story to show them I understood how they were feeling. Not only that, but I wanted them to know it was possible to overcome difficulties in life. I did this while also sharing the understanding that my pathway to triumph may not have been the best one.

That is why my story is a warning to anyone who has now read it. I don't want any child in the world to ever experience what I went through, and a large reason I had to endure what I did for so long was my own fault because I lacked the courage to talk to somebody. I did not have a teacher that I could go to and share my feelings, nor did my schools have counselors or other interventions set in place during my younger years when I probably needed them the most. However, I am declaring to you that it is okay to talk to somebody, so please do not hold it inside yourself. Share with a teacher, counselor, another adult, or a person you trust before it becomes too much to handle.

My greatest hope is that this book will prompt schools to create and use true anti-bullying strategies, and when I think about my own story, I believe it starts with building a community of young people that care and support one another no matter what their differences might be. When students are living in a positive environment amongst one another, they will always want to return to that feeling every day. Now that I am a teacher, this is exactly what I try to intentionally create in my own classroom.

On one final note, I would like to declare that I have completely forgiven Gene. What he did on that stage on a singular day for a small amount of time will never be forgotten for the rest of my life. Anybody who has read this story should never hold anything against Gene, but rather, look at what he did in the end to inspire you and others to do the same before time runs out. Ultimately, I have had to forgive myself for allowing the issues to last as long as they did, and it is now my duty to share this story and to use my platform as a teacher to make sure other kids never do what I did ever again.

Now I want to encourage those of you who are victims. You might be a direct or passive victim of bullying. Your bully might be a friend, sibling, parent, teacher, coach, co-worker, or somebody else. I wish you strength to push through and to persevere. Keep telling your story until someone listens and helps you deal with your bully. Don't hold in your pain like I did. Get it out and deal with it in a healthy manner. Don't carry it around with you like a weight pulling you down. My pain ruined what could have been a magical time in my life—all because I refused to get the appropriate help. Many other kids don't seek out support in the right ways either, and that is how suicides, as well as some school shootings, have occurred around the world.

Most of all, I also want to say to those of you who might be a "Gene," to be aware of how your opinions and actions can affect people negatively. It's a form of mental abuse that can last with someone an entire lifetime. You may think you are just kidding or being funny, but you are not. If you don't have something nice to say about someone, don't say anything. Instead, use your words for good. Challenge yourself to say something nice and complimentary to someone every day. And that subtle laugh you have? Stop it. Sometimes that minor chuckle is worse than some of the words you've said. Get into the habit of lifting people up and helping them see their talents in a positive way. You have the power to change the world with one word. Use that word for good.

And to one of the most important groups of people, those who give the "reassuring chuckle." Next time you catch yourself doing it like I had rudely done, think again if it's the right thing to do. I'll go ahead and answer that for you... it's not.

Lastly, I charge you with this: The power of a simple apology can change somebody's life. Take the opportunity to try it today. You will feel better for taking this simple step. An apology used early and often can change your outlook on life and make you feel better. Not to mention the person you are bestowing it upon. That person will respect you for coming forward and may even become your lifelong friend. And who doesn't need more friends? Many of you have heard the saying, "Actions speak louder than words," but I want you to know your words can resonate with others for years to come, so use them in the right way. I believe in you. Now, go believe in yourself.

RESOURCES

---

www.jugglingbullies.com

www.pacer.org/bullying/

www.stompoutbullying.org

www.stopbullying.gov

Nobully.org

www.napab.org

Teachantibullying.org

Ibpaworld.org

Befrienders.org

Suicidepreventionlifeline.org

Suicidepreventionlifeline.org/talk-to-someone-now

Suicide.org/international-suicide-hotlines.html

National Suicide Prevention Lifeline: 1-800-273-8255

Made in the USA
Monee, IL
18 June 2022

98243940R00135